Young People Leaving Care

Acknowledgements

It has been my good fortune to have worked with many first class people who have contributed significantly to the development of research, policy and practice about young people leaving care. My original research collaborator at Leeds University, over 30 years ago, was Kate Carey, and since then, and on moving to the University of York in 1995, Nina Biehal, Jasmine Clayden, Jo Dixon and Jim Wade, have all made substantial contributions. I also owe a debt to other colleagues at York who worked within the then Social Work Research and Development Unit, especially Ian Sinclair, my co-Director, and Leslie Hicks; excellent administrative support for this publication has been provided within the Social Policy Research Unit by Sally Pulleyn. For many years, and often 'over a pint, or two' many of the ideas contained within this book have been explored with John Pinkerton from Queen's University Belfast. He has offered wise external counsel.

I have also been greatly inspired by the members of the Transitions from Care to Adulthood International Research Group (INTRAC), which met in 2003, for the first time, bringing together researchers from Europe, the Middle East, Australia, Canada and the United States, and is still going strong. As well as contributing much to the group, Harriet Ward and Emily Munro from Loughborough University deserve credit for ensuring we are in the right place at the right time!

My knowledge of policy and practice has been enhanced greatly by working closely with the staff at the National Care Advisory Service (NCAS), including Dr Claire Baker, Linda Briheim-Crookall and Martin Hazlehurst, as well as the members of the National Benchmarking Forum; the latter have provided many of the practice examples contained within this publication.

Finally, I am indebted, as ever, to all those young people, whose lives have not been easy, but who have been prepared selflessly to share their lives with researchers, and who thus made this publication possible. It is of great pleasure to me that I meet up, from time to time, with the first young man I ever interviewed about leaving care. He is now 40, 'doing well' and settled with his partner and family.

Chapter 1

Introduction

> Coming out of care… I think it's becoming an adult, where you've got more responsibility, where you can go and find yourself a job, and be able to look after yourself, and not have to turn to them, and be able to be all right financially as well as mentally.

This book is about the journey travelled by young people from leaving care to becoming adult. For most young people today this journey takes place over time and includes a number of different but connected and reinforcing pathways: moving into accommodation of their choice; entering further or higher education, or training; finding satisfying employment; achieving good health and a positive sense of well-being, and, for some young people, becoming a parent. It is usually a time of expectation and excitement as well as apprehension and uncertainty.

As a group, young people leaving care may face more difficulties than other young people on these pathways to adulthood. Their journey may be shorter, more severe and often more hazardous than for those young people leaving their family home (Stein 2006a, 2009a). And they may have been burdened by earlier negative experiences of poor parenting, including maltreatment, and social disadvantage (Davies and Ward 2011; Rees *et al.* 2011). In addition, for some young people, the quality of care they have experienced may have failed to compensate them for past difficulties (Hannon, Wood and Bazalgette 2010; Sinclair *et al.* 2007).

In this context, it is not surprising that some young people find the journey to adulthood a great struggle, whilst other young people just survive, or get by, and make it, although the journey will often take a longer time. However, perhaps more surprising, is that some young people cope with the demands of the journey very well – they are well prepared to overcome the barriers they face on the pathways to adulthood (Stein 2005, 2008a). Understanding these differences in how young people cope and the progress they make – and what can assist young people during their journey, as well as the barriers they face – has important policy and practice implications for how the resilience of young people can be promoted during their journey from care to adulthood. An ecological perspective on resilience recognises the interaction between individual development and social context. What happens to young people in their families, schools and communities, before and when they are living in care, can all make a difference to how well they will cope with their journey to adulthood.

This book explores the journey from leaving care to adulthood through young people's main pathways – accommodation, careers, health and well-being. For each of these pathways this will include a review of what research studies reveal about the problems young people face during their journey, and how they may be assisted in meeting these challenges – or how the services they receive may help them fulfill their potential as young adults. This resilience approach will also be illustrated by examples of good practice and, in addition, make recommendations for improving policy and practice.

The quotations from young people leaving care that appear at the beginning of Chapters 1–10, and Chapter 12 (this also includes three quotations), and introduce Part 2 of the book, are from published research studies carried out between 1986 and 2011. These studies draw heavily on the views of young people who freely participated in the research (Stein and Carey 1986; Stein 1990; Biehal *et al.* 1995; Clayden and Stein 2005; Dixon and Stein 2005; Morgan and Lindsay 2006; Stein 2011).

Outline of the book

Although the focus of the book is on the English legal and policy context, it is informed by a body of international research findings that will be of relevance to supporting young people's pathways to adulthood in different legal contexts, including the different countries within the UK and internationally.

Part 1 of the book sets the policy and organisational context in which young people's pathways from care to adulthood take place. This begins in Chapter 2 by tracing the main developments in leaving care policy in England from the Children Act 1948, which introduced the first legal framework for after-care, to 2011, which saw the implementation of the Children and Young Persons Act 2008, and new Guidance and Regulations, *Planning Transition to Adulthood for Care Leavers* (Department for Education 2010a). Chapter 3 describes how the services that have been introduced to assist young people leaving care have been organised and classified, including the shift from their incorporation within generic childcare provision to specialist leaving care services, and the development of what can be seen as a 'corporate parenting case model', with legal responsibility held by personal advisers embedded within formalised intra- and inter-agency processes.

Part 2 of the book explores young people's main pathways from care to adulthood, beginning with accommodation. Chapter 4 discusses how young people can be assisted in finding and maintaining 'settled, safe, accommodation' of their choice. The contribution of carers and workers – foster and residential carers, kinship carers, birth families and housing workers – to this process, is described in Chapter 5. Chapter 6 addresses the issue of homelessness and how services can prevent young people leaving care becoming homeless as well as how they can be assisted out of homelessness.

Chapters 7 and 8 examine the career pathways of young people. This begins in Chapter 7, with an exploration of how young people's experiences of school education can lay the foundations of their subsequent careers. Chapter 8 focuses on their post-16 career pathways including entering vocational training, further or higher education and employment.

Chapters 9 and 10 discuss the health and well-being pathway. In Chapter 9 this includes an exploration of the physical and mental health of young people whilst they are living in care and after they leave. Chapter 10 focuses upon specific groups of young people whose needs or circumstances may result in them requiring additional support to enhance their well-being as they move on from care to adulthood. This includes disabled young people, young parents, young people from minority ethnic backgrounds, unaccompanied asylum-seeking young people, lesbian, gay, bisexual and trans-gendered young people, young offenders and young people who misuse substances.

Part 3 draws on the main themes and ideas which have informed this book. In Chapter 11 this includes social inclusion, participation, the life course, attachment, stability and social transition. Chapter 12, the concluding chapter, suggests that resilience gives coherence to these ideas and proposes a resilience framework across the life course of young people for understanding their experiences, and, through policy and practice interventions, improving their lives from leaving care to becoming adult.

PART I

SETTING THE CONTEXT

Those who cannot remember the past are condemned to repeat it.

(George Santayana 1905)

Chapter 2

The Making of Leaving Care Law and Policy, 1948–2012

When we leave care why should they stop caring?

This chapter describes the main developments in leaving care law and policy in England between 1948 and 2012.[1] It begins with the introduction of the Children Act 1948, which heralded the start of statutory after-care services, and describes the main landmarks in law and policy up to the introduction of the Children and Young Persons Act 2008 and *Planning Transition to Adulthood for Care Leavers* (Department for Education 2010a), the latter of which will be referred to as the *Transitions Guidance* in the text. Both came into force in April 2011. This account will explore how the legal and policy context has, over 60 years, helped or hindered young people during their journey from care to adulthood.

It is a story of how wider contextual influences, including opportunities and constraints, common to all young people, have interacted with a more parochial child welfare agenda, and the agency and actions of many, including young people in care themselves, in the making of leaving care policy. For example, the vulnerability of care leavers to unemployment and homelessness has to be considered in the wider context of major structural, economic and social policy changes affecting young people more generally in society at different historical moments. These changes have also to be understood in a wider global context which, in addition to youth unemployment and the impact of reductions in services, also includes responding to the

---

1   This chapter draws on and further develops material from earlier publications including Stein (1999, 2004, 2008b), as referenced.

human consequences of unaccompanied young people seeking asylum (Pinkerton 2011; Wade 2011).

Children's Departments and after-care: 1948–1968

The Children Act 1948, based upon the recommendations of the Curtis Committee, created the new Children's Departments. A single Committee and Department, was for the first time, to have the responsibility for the continuous care of all children deprived of a normal home life. The reforming spirit of 1945 and Labour's new social democratic politics provided the ideological climate for the acceptance of welfare policies, which reflected a more humane and liberal approach than had gone before. The Poor Law, which operated in tandem with the harsh morality theory of the Charity Organisation Society, in classifying the 'deserving' from the 'undeserving', and religious and biological determinism, had all condemned the poor.

In keeping with the new thinking, Section 12 of the Children Act 1948 finally broke with the Poor Law status of 'less eligibility' for children in care under which so many children had suffered. The Poor Law mentality, which shaped much residential childcare during the 1930s, was captured by a Home Office Inspector's report:

> In residential homes, both statutory and voluntary staff were found to be treating the children as 'lower orders' who did not deserve the ordinary standards of civilised living. In one home the windows lacked curtains for fear that the children would wipe their noses on them; they were not provided with handkerchiefs. In an Anglican convent home menstruation was not to be mentioned and the girls were given nothing to cope with it so they tore strips from their sheets and face towels. Children had no clothes of their own; often they were assembled in height order and marched to a counter where they received the next day's garments. (Cited in Barnardo's 1987, p.9)

The Children Act 1948 gave local authorities a new duty to 'further best interests...and afford opportunities for proper development of character and abilities' and 'make such use of facilities and services available for children in the care of their own parents' (The Children Act 1948: Section 12(1) (2)). This included a new legal framework in regard to the after-care of young people – a duty to advise and befriend; a power to accommodate; and powers in respect of providing financial

By the beginning of the 1970s it seemed social work had developed a strong professional identity and a clear vision of the future. The growing influence and power of social work was exemplified by the key role of childcare experts in shaping the Children and Young Persons Act 1969, and, by its contribution to the Seebohm Report, in determining the future organisation of social services. But at the same time as the internal dynamic for professional unity and growth was reaching its peak the external context was changing. The consensus surrounding the belief in the good society was evaporating.

The rediscovery of poverty, greater recognition of a range of social problems including inner-city deprivation, homelessness, ethnic conflict and educational under-achievement, combined with challenges to traditional forms of authority and authority relations by new pressure groups and social movements, to point to a far more uncertain future. A professional culture which had stabilised itself around a psychodynamic world view and which focused exclusively upon the pathology of the individual, or family, as both a cause and solution, was being challenged. The new curriculum included anti-psychiatry, deviance theory and Marxism, the new practice welfare rights, community work and advocacy. The total equalled radical social work (Pearson 1975).

More specifically, the reorganisation of the personal social services and the introduction of the Children and Young Persons Act 1969, both in 1971, far from leading to a comprehensive after-care service within the new departments, resulted in the decline of specialist after-care work in many local authorities. The end of the probation service's involvement in after-care, with no commensurate transfer of resources to the new Social Services Departments, as envisaged by Seebohm, the replacement of approved school orders with the new all-purpose care orders, and the related redesignation of approved schools as Community Homes with Education, all contributed to the demise of the specialist after-care officer.

Specialist work with young people, either living in children's homes (now designated Community Homes) or after they left care, also became a very low priority among the new front-line generic social workers – and many fieldwork practitioners were new and untrained following the post-Seebohm bureaucratisation of social services. Care leavers became a forgotten group. But it was not too long before their voices were heard. Against the wider background of the major social changes outlined above, as well as the emergence of an embryonic children's rights movement, there was a reawakening of leaving care in the professional and political consciousness.

From as early as 1973 small groups of young people living in care came together to talk about their experiences of living in children's homes, of being on 'the receiving end'. Local 'in care' groups, the *Who Cares?* project, Black and In Care and the National Association of Young People in Care, in different ways, began to unlock the feelings and views of young people about care, and in particular, the connections between their lives in care and their lives after care (Stein 2011). A major theme that emerged from the voices of young people was their lack of power over their lives, for example, in relation to their use of money, their attendance at their own reviews, their opportunities to shop, cook and generally to participate while in care. And the dependency created by care was related to their fears about leaving care.

> They do everything for you, I don't really know how to look after myself... I want to get out but then I don't want to because I don't have anybody outside... If you live with your parents you have a choice whether you leave home or not. In care you get kicked out, you don't feel you belong once you have left. (Young people's views cited in Stein 2011, p.23)

A major gap in our knowledge in the post-war period was due to the absence of any research into leaving care. But this was beginning to change from the second half of the 1970s with the publication of mainly small-scale descriptive accounts and studies (Burgess 1981; First Key 1987; Godek 1976; Kahan 1976; Lupton 1985; Millham *et al.* 1986; Morgan-Klein 1985; Mulvey 1977; Page and Clark 1977; Stein and Ellis 1983; Stein and Carey 1986; Stein and Maynard 1985; Triseliotis 1980). The main impact of these studies was to highlight for the first time the problems and challenges experienced by young people leaving care. These findings also showed that many young people left care at just 16 years of age and were expected to live independently.

Changes in childcare law and practice introduced during the 1970s (as a result of the Children and Young Persons Act 1969), contributed to this. For while the old approved school orders, parental rights resolutions and fit person orders combined legal prescription and high-level committee authority with normative expectations in determining the age of discharge from care, discretionary welfare, embodied in the new care order, was far more subject to individual social work judgement and external constraint – the latter including pragmatic concerns, such as the pressure on residential care places. An ironic situation given the hopes riding on the new welfare thinking to contribute to a more needs-led practice.

The low priority afforded to these young people in the new generic Social Services Departments has already been commented upon. There was to be little improvement in after-care services during the 1970s and early 1980s, as against a background of successive child abuse inquiries, child protection work increasingly became the main preoccupation (Parton 1985). In addition, while an emerging welfare model had gone hand in hand with the commitment of the pre-Seebohm childcare officer to assist these young people, radical social work and the new curriculum, including the developing children's rights discourse, was a far more contradictory force. It did, as has been argued, provide a climate for the reawakening of leaving care in the political and professional consciousness, particularly through its support for advocacy and in-care groups. But it was a crude practice nourished on a very basic diet of Marxism (Pearson 1975). It didn't want to know about residential care, about more bricks in the wall. And even less about those behind the wall.

Also, subsequent policy developments during this period, however progressive in themselves, did not serve these young people well. The persistence of the institutional critique and the closely linked and enduring popularity of community care, both underpinned by a rare academic and political consensus, the rise of the permanency movement to greatly increase the use of adoption and fostering, and the managerial and professional drive to prevent and divert young people from entering care, all reinforced the same message: residential care is bad. And it was – and a lot worse than was realised at the time given subsequent revelations of physical and sexual abuse (Colton 2002; House of Commons 2000; Stein 2006b; Utting 1991, 1997).

During these years, residential care increasingly operated in a climate of denial and welfare planning blight, as well as in a philosophical and theoretical void. But neither were young people leaving foster care seen as 'leaving care' in a formal sense – the assumption being that they would continue to be supported by their foster carers. In this context, little thought was given to preparation for leaving foster care or to the type and extent of after-care support needed. Social Services Departments were thus, in the main, unprepared for the major changes in society and in social legislation that were to have such a significant impact upon the lives of care leavers.

From the late 1970s onwards there have been profound economic and social changes, changes described and analysed as post-Fordism and by the other 'post' – post modernism (Clarke 1996). And, while the former captures the processes of economic reorganisation in advanced industrial societies, the latter suggests a new post – or late? – modern era of fundamental and complex transformations in the social, economic, cultural and technological spheres (Giddens 1991). The decline in traditional industries, the development in new technologies and the dramatic rise in youth unemployment during the 1980s had a major impact upon the lives of many young people. And, while in the past a highly stratified job market had been able to provide opportunities for all, whatever their level of education, the low levels of educational attainment of most care leavers now left them ill-prepared to compete in an increasingly competitive youth labour market. As a consequence a high proportion of care leavers were unemployed and dependent on some form of benefit and therefore living in, or on, the margins of poverty (Stein 1990).

In March 1980 the plight of homeless young people first became a headline story following the media take-up of Christian Wolmar's article 'Out of care' that appeared in Shelter's magazine *Roof* (Wolmar 1980). The author's combative exposé of homeless ex-care young people in London, drifting from hostels to squats to railway arches, led directly to Shelter setting up Homebase (which later became First Key, then the National Leaving Care Advisory Service, and currently the National Care Advisory Service) in response to the inadequate housing provision being made by local authorities for young people leaving care (Wolmar 1980). Following Wolmar's revelations, two studies, published in 1981, showed that over a third of single homeless people had experienced local authority care (Department of the Environment 1981; Scottish Council for Single Homeless 1981).

The actions and self-organisation of young people themselves, the findings from researchers, the increased awareness by practitioners and managers of the problems faced by care leavers, and the campaigning activities of Shelter and First Key, provided the momentum for a change to the law in relation to leaving care, which had remained much the same as the Children Act 1948.

The opportunity was provided by a major reform of childcare law being carried out during the 1980s. However, after all the evidence had been considered, and the law reviewed, there was only to be one obligatory change (a duty) in respect of leaving care between the

Children Act 1989 and the 'old' Children Act 1948. This was a new duty, under Section 24(1), 'to advise, assist and befriend young people who are looked after with a view to promote their welfare when they cease to be looked after'.

New permissive powers were introduced under Section 24, 'to advise and befriend other young people under 21 who were cared for away from home' – thus widening the target group for after-care support, and under Section 27, 'the power to request the help of other local authorities, including any local housing authority to enable them to comply with their duties to provide accommodation'. But other than that there was far more of the old than the new in the 1989 Act – the old duty to advise and befriend young people under 21 who were looked after remained, as did the permissive powers to provide financial assistance.

In fairness, it could be argued that the Children Act 1989 introduced a far more progressive legal framework as a general context for care leavers, given the close connections between the lives of young people in families, in care and after care. In this sense, the new provisions for family support services, for the inclusion of children with disabilities, for the recognition of culture, language, racial origin and religion, for consultative rights, for the accommodation of children in need and for new rights to complain, were all to be welcomed. But this should not detract from the way that social work policy and practice failed many of these young people during much of this period.

The implementation of the Children Act 1989

The Children Act 1989 could not have been implemented at a more difficult time for care leavers – the virtual end of the traditional job market, shrinking housing options, major cuts in welfare benefits and reduced expenditure on public services.

The reform of social security (by the Social Security Acts 1986 and 1988) based on the 'guarantee' of youth training and the assumption that families should take greater financial responsibilities for their young people, ended income support for 16 and 17 year olds, except in severe hardship, and abolished 'householder status' for under 25s, by the introduction of lower rates of income support for this age group. Although campaigning activity by care leavers resulted in exceptions for them to receive income support at 16 and 17 for limited periods, the differential age rates of income support remained in place, resulting in demands on social services to provide 'top-up' payments in order to prevent young people from experiencing extreme poverty, deprivation and homelessness (Stein 1990).

From the mid-1980s, in response to the increasingly desperate situation facing many young people leaving care, some voluntary organisations and local authorities – but by no means all – pioneered specialist leaving care schemes and projects (see Chapter 3). Planning for the 1989 Act also increased the profile and awareness of leaving care within many local authorities and the introduction of specialist schemes was seen by social services as a way of meeting their new legal responsibilities under the Children Act 1989.

For some local authorities, the 1989 Act provided the legislative framework for a comprehensive range of leaving care services, through the provision of specialist leaving care schemes, integrated within an overall general childcare strategy linking care and after-care (Biehal *et al.* 1995; Stein and Wade 2000). However, the more general picture in England and Wales was of great variation in the funding, range and quality of service provision, as well the complex, inconsistent and discouraging wider social policy framework – confirmed by a wide range of sources including research findings, the Social Service Inspectorate, and the Action on Aftercare Consortium. Research findings from Scotland and Northern Ireland revealed a similar picture (Biehal *et al.* 1995; Broad 1998; Department of Health 1997; Dixon and Stein 2005; Garnett 1992; Pinkerton and McCrea 1999; Stein, Pinkerton and Kelleher 2000).

The Children (Leaving Care) Act 2000

The Labour government, elected in 1997, in its response to the Children's Safeguards Review, following the revelations of widespread abuse in children's homes, committed itself to legislate for new and stronger duties for care leavers. Sir William Utting, who chaired the Review, had drawn attention to the plight of 16-year-old care leavers, 'unsupported financially and emotionally, without hope of succour in distress' (Utting 1997). In addition, the research evidence cited above was persuasive.

The proposed changes, detailed in the consultation document, *Me, Survive, Out There?* were to build upon Labour's modernisation programme for children's services in England (Department of Health 1999). This included the Quality Protects initiative introduced in 1998 in England, providing substantial central government funding linked to specific service objectives. In relation to young people leaving care, Objective 5 was to 'ensure that young people leaving care, as they enter adulthood, are not isolated and participate socially and economically as citizens'. Three performance indicators linked to this objective were 'for young people looked after at the age of 16, to maximise the number engaged in education, training or employment at 19; to maximise the number of young people leaving care after their sixteenth birthday who are still in touch…on their nineteenth birthday; to maximise the number of young people leaving care on or after their sixteenth birthday who have suitable accommodation at the age of 19' (Department of Health 2000, Objective 5.0, 5.1–5.3).

Also, in England, wider government initiatives to combat social exclusion, including the introduction of the Connexions Service, and initiatives to tackle youth homelessness, under-achievement in education, employment and training, and young parenthood were intended to impact upon care leavers (SEU 1998, 1999). Indeed, the changing economic climate combined with the restructuring of post-16-year-old education and training resulted in reductions in youth unemployment – although there continued to be regional variations, as well as stratification by class, gender, disability and ethnicity, and the continued expansion of low-paid jobs in the service industries: more opportunities and more risks?

Against this background, the Children (Leaving Care) Act 2000 was introduced in England and Wales in October 2001. Its main aims are to delay young people's transitions from care until they are prepared and ready to leave; strengthen the assessment, preparation and planning for leaving care; provide better personal support for young people after care; and to improve the financial arrangements for care leavers.

In meeting these aims the Act's key responsibilities are: a duty to assist young people until they are 21, or up to the age of 24 if they are in approved programmes of education and training; a duty to assess and meet the needs of young people in and leaving care; pathway planning; financial support; maintenance in suitable accommodation; and a duty to keep in touch by the 'responsible authority'.

The Children (Leaving Care) Act 2000 provided an opportunity for improving services and thus the level of resources for young people leaving care. Surveys of the work of leaving care teams carried out before and after the Act point to improvements in financial support, increases in the proportion of young people entering post-16 education and related reductions in those not in education, employment or training (Broad 1998, 1999, 2005). There has also been a strengthening and clarification of roles towards care leavers through needs assessments and pathway planning, and a greater involvement in inter-agency work (Hai and Williams 2004). However, the research evidence also reveals a wide degree of variation in the funding, range and quality of services between local authorities (Broad 2005). The impact of the Act upon young people's pathways to adulthood is explored in subsequent chapters.

Every Child Matters and Care Matters

In 2003, the government published their Green Paper, *Every Child Matters* (Department for Education and Skills 2003). It identified four key themes: increasing the focus on supporting parents and carers; early intervention and effective protection; strengthening accountability and the integration of services at all levels; and workforce reform. The government's aim for all children and young people, whatever their background or circumstances, was to have the support they need to improve outcomes in five key areas: being healthy, staying safe, enjoying and achieving, making a positive contribution and achieving economic well-being. Published alongside the government's response to the report into the death of Victoria Climbié, *Every Child Matters* resulted in a major consultation exercise and review of children's services, leading to the Children Act 2004, the latter strengthening the legal framework to protect and safeguard children from harm. In November 2004, *Every Child Matters: Change for Children* (Department for Education and Skills 2004) identified new ways in which all organisations involved with children and young people could work better together. In 2005, *Youth Matters* (Department for Education and Skills 2005) set out the government's priorities to support young people outside of schools, including action to give young people more say in how their needs are met.

In October 2006, the government published their Green Paper, *Care Matters: Transforming the Lives of Children and Young People in Care* (Department for Education and Skills 2006), against the background of continuing evidence of poor educational and career outcomes for children and young people living in and leaving care (Wade and Dixon 2006). The wide range of responses to this document, including a major consultation exercise with young people in care, conducted by the What Makes A Difference project, contributed to the White Paper, *Care Matters: Time for Change* (Department for Education and Skills 2007), published in June 2007. Its main proposals led to the Children and Young Persons Act 2008 and the *Care Matters* implementation plan.

The Children and Young Persons Act 2008 and *Planning Transition to Adulthood for Care Leavers*

The coalition government came to power in 2010 and they have proceeded with the implementation of the Children and Young Persons Act 2008 and the introduction of the *Transitions Guidance*, both from April 2011. The main provisions of the Children and Young Persons Act 2008 are: first, to ensure that young people have a statutory review, to take into account their views before moving – so they do not leave care before they are ready; second, their entitlement to a personal adviser will be extended to care leavers under the age of 25 who wish to resume an education and training programme, and, third, a requirement (a duty) for local authorities to provide a Higher Education Bursary.

It is intended that the *Transitions Guidance*, in conjunction with the implementation of the Children and Young Persons Act 2008, will strengthen the current legal, policy and practice framework, and that this will contribute to a 'levelling up' of services, as there is evidence both from official data and research based on the views of young people leaving care of variation in the range and quality of leaving care services (Department for Education 2011a, b; Morgan and Lindsay 2012).

These new responsibilities are being implemented at the same time as reductions in local authority expenditure and the funding of third sector services, changes in housing and welfare benefits, changes to financial support for students and rising youth unemployment. The coalition's proposals for public services also include an Open Public Services White Paper which sets out five principles for modernising public services: increasing choice wherever possible; public services should be decentralised to the lowest appropriate level; public service should be open to a range of providers; ensuring fair access to public services; and public services should be accountable to users and taxpayers (NCB 2011a).

In this context they are piloting 'Payment By Results' (PBR) and Social Impact Bonds (SIBs), as part of a wider shift towards outcome-based commissioning and social investment. The National Council for Voluntary Youth Services (NCVYS) define PBR:

> This is where a commissioning body agrees to fund a provider on the basis that they will achieve particular agreed outcomes, rather then deliver particular outputs. PBR refers to a system in which public service commissioners pay providers according to specified outcomes as opposed to paying for services at the start of a contract. (NCVYS 2011, p.2)

SIBs are seen by the coalition as a way of reducing the financial risk to organisations, by encouraging investors to fund new initiatives to reduce social problems. The three main elements are: up-front monetary investment, for example from local authorities, commercial investors, philanthropists or foundations; the provision of a service to assist a group; and commitments by the investors to make payments linked to improved outcomes achieved by the group – for example, repayment of the original investment and an extra percentage agreed return, sustained by reduced costs.

NCVYS has identified a number of potential problems with PBR and SIBs including: the cost implications for smaller cash-strapped voluntary organisations in having to wait for funding, although this may be eased by social investment; whether 'results' can be measured over a short period of time – given that the impact of interventions with vulnerable young people may not be realised until their adulthood; the fact that the latter could lead to a focus on measuring short-term results, excluding work with the most vulnerable young people; and whether it is possible to identify the specific services which achieve results – with vulnerable young people a lot of the work is multi-agency (NCVYS 2011). All these issues would have implications for leaving care services if PBR were introduced.

In respect of the impact of current policy, there is evidence from 27 local authorities surveyed by the National Care Advisory Service (NCAS) in March 2011 that over half reported planned funding cuts in leaving care services (ranging between 7% and 15%), which would lead to higher case loads and make it difficult to implement the *Transitions Guidance*, especially keeping in regular contact and supporting young people wanting to pursue education and training after 21 years of age (National Care Advisory Service 2011a).

In addition, most authorities (80%) reported seeing the impact of cuts to complementary local services and provision, including education, training and employment support, which they use to support care leavers. Just under a third of authorities reported that the cuts were as yet unknown (National Care Advisory Service 2011a). In their report they comment:

> Over the last ten years, since the introduction of the Children (Leaving Care) Act 2000, services for care leavers in local authorities have developed greatly. Local authorities have sought to meet the needs of their young people in different ways and many varied models of services have resulted, with different staffing levels and funding. The impact of reduced budgets will therefore not be uniform. However, our findings reveal a general pattern of great uncertainty within services and concern about the capacity to continue to support young people effectively and implement the new guidance and regulations. (National Care Advisory Service 2011a, p.1)

The implications of the Children and Young Persons Act 2008 and the *Transitions Guidance*, as well as policy changes introduced by the coalition government which impact upon young people's pathways from care to adulthood will be explored in the subsequent chapters.

Summary points

- The Children Act 1948 introduced duties and powers in respect of the after-care of young people which laid the foundation of leaving care services. It was significant that the age of leaving care, at 18 years of age, mirrored the normative age and process of young people moving on from families.

- The reorganisation of the personal social services and changes in childcare law, introduced in 1971, led to a decline of specialist after-care provision. These changes also led to young people leaving care earlier, often as young as 16, whereas young people were remaining with their families until their early 20s.

- From the mid-1970s the findings from researchers highlighted for the first time the problems faced by young people leaving care, and these findings, combined with sustained campaigning, including the actions and self-organisation of young people themselves and increased awareness by practitioners, provided a momentum for change to the law.

- The Children Act 1989, which was introduced in October 1991, although very progressive in many respects, was far weaker in relation to leaving care. Other than a new duty to prepare young people, the Act, in the main, only extended permissive powers.

- The Children Act 1989 was also implemented at the most difficult time for care leavers – with the decline of the traditional job market for young people, shrinking housing options, major cuts in welfare benefits and reduced expenditure on public services. However, the Act did raise the profile of the vulnerability of care leavers and led directly to the introduction of more specialist leaving care schemes.

- Research carried out during the 1990s highlighted the weakness of the discretionary powers contained within the 1989 Act, as well as the complex, inconsistent and discouraging wider social policy framework for young people, particularly in relation to benefits and housing.

- The Children (Leaving Care) Act was introduced in October 2001. It led to an increased take-up of further education, reductions in the numbers of young people not in education, employment and training, a strengthening of leaving care responsibilities and improved funding for leaving care teams.

- *Every Child Matters* introduced normative outcomes for all children and young people, whatever their background or circumstances – connecting the progress and outcomes of care leavers with other young people.

- Proposals to improve outcomes for young people living in and leaving care were contained within the 2007 White Paper *Care Matters: Time for Change*. This highlighted the long-standing issue of young people leaving care before they were prepared and ready, and the contrast with the age at which most young people left home. Its proposals formed the basis of the Children and Young Persons Act 2008.

- In October 2010 *Planning Transition to Adulthood for Care Leavers* (*Transitions Guidance*) was published, updating the Children Act 1989 Guidance and Regulations.

- The Children and Young Persons Act 2008 and the *Transitions Guidance* were implemented by the coalition government from April 2011 at the same time as cuts and planned changes in services, and evidence of variation in the range and quality of services.

- The coalition government is also piloting changes in funding of public services, including PBR and SIBs, which potentially could be extended to leaving care services.

Chapter 3

The Organisation of Leaving Care Services

I've learnt to live out of care – with a back-up team.

This chapter describes the development and organisation of services to assist young people leaving care, focusing, in the main, on the period between the implementation of the Children Act 1989 and the introduction of the *Transitions Guidance* in 2011. This will bring together the reasons for the introduction of leaving care services, the different ways leaving care schemes and projects have been organised and classified, and a description of the range of work they undertake in supporting young people on their pathways to adulthood.

The origins of leaving care services

The introduction of specialist services for care leavers – those carrying the label 'leaving care' – can in the main be traced back to the mid-1980s. Maureen Stone, in her 1989 survey of 33 specialist schemes, found that only one scheme was in existence in 1978 and the majority, over three-quarters, started in 1985 or later (Stone 1990). But the designation 'leaving care' does not mark the beginning of leaving care services. Schemes, programmes and efforts to assist young people leaving care are as old as the childcare services themselves, whether they were unrecognised as part of the ordinary and informal responsibilities of foster carers, or more organised, such as the early work placement schemes pioneered by Barnardo in the nineteenth century. As detailed in Chapter 2, following the introduction of the new Children's Departments in 1948, 'working boys hostels', 'mother and baby homes', lodging houses, and designated probation, after-care and childcare officers were provided in many areas to support young people after care.

Also, as discussed in Chapter 2, the reorganisation of the personal social services and the introduction of the Children and Young Persons Act 1969, both in 1971, led to a decline of specialist after-care work in many local authorities. In respect of the former, the new generic all-purpose social workers, the high priority given to child protection work and the community and diversionary focus of radical social work contributed to the neglect of care leavers and their after-care. As regards the latter, discretionary welfare embodied in the new care orders introduced under the 1969 Act, led to a lowering of the age at which young people left care.

The Children Act 1989 and leaving care services

During the 1980s, against a wider background of major economic and social change – contributing to high levels of unemployment, a shortage of housing and reductions in social security – the desperation of many of these young people, some homeless and destitute, was highlighted. Campaigning organisations, including Shelter, researchers, practitioners working with young people and, not least, young care leavers themselves, all made their voices heard. This led to the introduction in some areas of specialist leaving care schemes and projects, as well as providing the momentum for change to existing legislation to assist care leavers.

Different schemes were identified in the early literature by service delivery and philosophy (Stein 1991). Service delivery models included: non-specialist service provision carried out by mainstream childcare social workers, which, the results of a 1992 survey indicate, was the main form of provision at that time; specialist leaving care teams; supported accommodation projects; and youth and community work approaches (First Key 1992).

The main difference in philosophy, reflected in the programme content, identified in the early literature was between independence and inter-dependence models. The rationale of independence schemes was that young people should be trained to manage on their own from 16 onwards primarily through instruction in practical survival skills and by coping with minimum support:

> Some of these units see independence training like a domestic combat course: young people being marked out of ten on a checklist for each activity, from opening a tin of baked beans to folding sheets and then

'passing out' when they have reached the required standard. (Stein and Carey 1986, pp.157–158)

In contrast, inter-dependence models saw leaving care more as a psychosocial transition, a high priority being placed on inter-personal skills, developing self-esteem and confidence, and receiving ongoing support after a young person leaves care (Stein and Carey 1986).

The introduction of specialist schemes and projects was seen by Social Services Departments as a way of meeting their leaving care responsibilities under the Children Act 1989. Research carried out between 1990 and 1995 showed that they provided a focused response to the core needs of care leavers – for assistance with accommodation, personal and social support, finance and help with careers (Biehal *et al.* 1995). Their work, post-Children Act 1989, included:

- a contribution to policy development and the co-ordination of leaving care services within local areas

- the development of a flexible range of resource options for young people, and, in some instances, co-ordinating access to them, especially in relation to further and higher education, employment and training, housing and financial support

- the development of inter-agency links to ensure an integrated approach to assisting young people

- the provision of advice, information and direct individual and group-based personal support to young people, including those preparing for leaving care and those living independently in the community

- the provision of training and consultancy services for staff and carers

- the monitoring and evaluating of their services.

Biehal *et al.* suggested a three-dimensional basis for classifying scheme distinctiveness (Biehal *et al.* 1995): first, how schemes compare in their approaches to service delivery, in terms of perspective, methods of working and the extent to which their work is young person demand-led – engaging and involving young people – or social work-planned; second, comparison between schemes in terms of the providing agency – whether statutory or voluntary – including their culture and organisational, management and staffing structures; and, third, the contribution made by specialist schemes to the development of leaving care policy within their local authority areas.

Broad's 1996 English survey of 46 specialist leaving care projects working with 3308 young people found that the majority of these projects, nearly two-thirds, started after the Children Act 1989 was enacted. Just under a third were provided and funded entirely by local authorities, just over a third provided by voluntary organisations but funded from a range of different sources, and a third jointly funded by local authorities and voluntary organisations (Broad 1998, 1999).

The results of a 1999 English survey of best practice in leaving care (based on responses from 42 local authorities) suggest that despite the diversity of service types, four main models of authority-wide provision were common at that time (Stein and Wade 2000):

1. A 'non-specialist service', where responsibility for delivering a service rests primarily with field social workers, sometimes in collaboration with young people's carers.

2. A 'centrally organised specialist service', consisting of a centrally organised team of leaving care workers providing an authority-wide service, primarily to care leavers.

3. A 'dispersed specialist service', where individual specialist leaving care workers are attached to area-based fieldwork teams.

4. A 'centrally organised integrated service', a model that attempts to provide an integrated service for a wider range of vulnerable young people 'in need', such as homeless young people, young offenders and young disabled people. Integration is facilitated through a multi-agency management and staffing model.

A survey of 33 London boroughs added to this picture (Vernon 2000). This research identified two different types of specialist teams: first, a specialist dual system arrangement. This entailed the young person being referred to the specialist leaving care team, but with statutory responsibility being retained by the locality social worker. The leaving care specialists would provide the preparation and after-care support, without the disadvantage of the 'authority' tag, seen to be associated with statutory responsibilities. Most of these teams were located in their own premises and moving on was seen as part of the 'rite de passage' for the young person. This was reflected in the name of the projects, for example, the Independence Plus Project and the Young Person's Independence Service.

Second, looked-after adolescent teams, which acquired statutory responsibility for the young person, and in the main, worked with young people from the age of 15 upwards. The rational for the setting up of these teams was to attract staff that had a commitment to working with adolescents and prevent the delay of cross-referral built into the system described above. The London survey also cited contractual arrangements with voluntary service providers and teams for vulnerable young people – the integrated service model – identified in the best practice servey above.

Leaving care teams and the Children (Leaving Care) Act 2000

The Children (Leaving Care) Act 2000 was implemented in October 2001, and Broad in his 2002–2003 survey was able to identify 300 leaving care teams working in England and Wales (Broad 2003a, 2003b). He surveyed 52 of these leaving care teams, working with 6953 young people, representing one in six English and Welsh local authorities. The survey found that nearly two-thirds of the teams were established before the introduction of the Act, including half of them before 1995. Just over a quarter were established in anticipation of, or immediately after the introduction of the Act.

Local authorities provided three-quarters of the teams and the remaining quarter was split almost evenly between teams run solely by voluntary organisations and those jointly provided by local authorities and voluntary organisations. In comparison with his 1998 profile, this shows significantly more local authority and fewer voluntary and joint providers, suggesting a greater role for local authorities in the implementation of the Children (Leaving Care) Act 2000.

Broad's survey found that the 52 teams employed 595 staff, the equivalent of a ratio of 12 young people to one staff member, compared with a 15:1 ratio in the 1998 survey. A quarter of the staff was identified as specialist staff who were appointed as 'personal advisers' under the Children (Leaving Care) Act, and just under half as 'specialist leaving care social workers'. The remaining staff was identified as 'other specialist' and this included education and employment workers (11.1%) and health staff (2.1%).

The main work of the teams surveyed included assistance with education, employment and training, accommodation and health; financial support; work with specific groups of young people, including young disabled people, unaccompanied asylum-seeking young people, and young people on remand; anti-discriminatory practice; work in supporting post-16 placements; and acting as personal advisers carrying out needs assessment and pathway planning under the 2000 Act (Broad 2003a).

Research into the implementation of the first two years of the Children (Leaving Care) Act in eight London boroughs identifies significant changes in the structures, policies and resources of leaving care services during this period (Hai and Williams 2004).

First of all, this included the development of specialist 16-plus leaving care services in seven of the areas, with workers having full case management responsibility for eligible, relevant and former relevant young people under the 2000 Act, case responsibility passing to the team in the young person's 16th year. In the remaining authority the leaving and after-care service was contracted out to an external voluntary agency.

A second major change was the greater involvement of staff from other agencies, either located within the team, or attached to them in a named capacity. This included staff from Connexions, health and mental health services, housing, education, drugs services, children's rights, psychology, family mediation, nursing, benefits, outreach, befriending and mentoring. On the basis of interviews with staff and young people the research found that these arrangements allowed the social workers with case responsibility to concentrate on carrying out the statutory requirements of the 2000 Act, while the specialist staff were able to co-ordinate their agency response, such as housing, education and health.

Third, the introduction of central government ring-fenced money had resulted in both better funding of services, including increased staffing levels and greater financial freedom to meet the needs of young people, especially to respond to crises and problems. Overall, the study saw the Children (Leaving Care) Act 2000 as contributing to the increased profile of leaving care services within the London authorities (Hai and Williams 2004). However, services were not seen as improving for all care leavers. Young disabled people were described as a 'hidden group among care leavers'. They were likely to be dealt with by specialist disabilities teams and be denied access to mainstream leaving care services – reflecting the division in services, and their underlying narratives, identified by Priestley, Rabiee and Harris (2003).

Dixon and Stein's policy survey of all Scottish local authorities (response rate of 97%) carried out during 2000 revealed that just over two-thirds of authorities had a specialist team or specialist staff with direct responsibility for providing 'through-care and after-care' services. Just under two-thirds of those teams were centrally located and nearly three-quarters were managed and funded by the local Social Work Departments. The remaining specialist teams included those jointly managed and funded by the Social Work Departments and the voluntary sector or other external agencies. All of these were centrally located. The Centrally Organised Specialist team was the main specialist model – there was no evidence of geographically dispersed specialist staff within fieldwork teams. Just over a half of these teams or specialist staff provided a service to all eligible young people within their authorities, the others provided services for young people not able to live at or return home. Over half reported having a written description of the services provided by the team (Dixon and Stein 2005).

The Scottish study also showed that just under a third of Social Work Departments had no specialist team or staff with direct responsibility for providing through-care and after-care services. Most of these departments responded that field social workers, residential social workers and foster carers were involved in providing these services. However, most respondents were unable to identify the numbers of staff involved and less than half had a written description of the range of through-care and after-care services provided. Generally, non-specialist services were being provided in larger rural areas, or in geographical areas, where the numbers of young people eligible to receive formal through-care and after-care were smaller (Dixon and Stein 2005).

In addition to the main models of authority-wide provision detailed above there is a very wide range of projects, many provided by the voluntary sector, which provide services for care leavers or other groups of vulnerable young people including care leavers – although, as suggested below they are increasingly incorporated into local leaving care services through formal agreements. Their work includes: improving preparation; providing an appropriate range of accommodation; tailoring individual support; accessing education, training and employment; assisting with health and well-being; improving the participation of care leavers; providing clear information for care leavers; and monitoring, evaluation and future planning.

evidence that leaving care teams and personal advisers are seen by many young people in a very positive light, being singled out in research on *Care Leavers' Perspectives on Public Services* (Consumer Focus 2011) 'as offering a responsive personalised service' (p.10). The corporate parenting case model, as discussed above, has evolved over time, and learnt from earlier deficiencies in meeting the diverse needs of care leavers. However, as research based upon young people's views shows, significant challenges remain in tackling territorial injustices – in raising the level of 'poor' services to that achieved by 'good' services (Morgan and Lindsay 2012). This issue will be explored in Chapter 11.

Summary points

- Designated 'leaving care' schemes have, in the main, been introduced since the mid-1980s – although as Chapter 2 documents, specialist leaving care services go much further back in time. A case of rediscovery rather than innovation!

- Specialist schemes have been developed to respond to the core needs of care leavers for assistance on their main pathways to adulthood, including accommodation, education, employment and training, finance, health and well-being, and personal and social support.

- Evaluations in the UK suggest there are differences in terms of philosophy, service delivery, the culture of the providing agency and in their contribution to policy development.

- Models of authority-wide provision include: non-specialist; central or dispersed specialist; and integrated provision for vulnerable young people. There is also a wide range of projects either aimed at assisting care leavers or aimed at other vulnerable young people including care leavers.

- The introduction of the Children (Leaving) Care Act 2000, the Children and Young Persons Act 2008 and Guidance and Regulations on *Transitions to Adulthood for Care Leavers* has led to the development of a 'corporate parenting case model'.

- This model has resulted in more clearly defined structures and defined roles and responsibilities, more formalised multi-agency work and in the increased profile of leaving care services. Many young people have a very positive view of leaving care teams and the support they receive from personal advisers, although there is evidence of variation in the quality of services.

PART 2

PATHWAYS TO ADULTHOOD

It's not being in care, what matters is when you've got to leave it…it frightens me…thinking, where am I gonna be next year. I'm not gonna be here, where am I gonna be?

It's difficult for young people moving out of care – you still carry the memories with you. I just want to make something of my life… I want as normal a life as any other person. I'd have a job, a family, a car and my own family around me if I needed support.

Chapter 4

Being in Settled, Safe Accommodation

> My main worry about leaving care – not being able to settle anywhere, having to keep moving around.

For most young people today, being in settled, safe accommodation of their choice represents an important landmark on their journey to adulthood. However, for young people leaving care, achieving this goal may be more difficult than for other young people. They may feel they have been forced to leave care before they are ready, often at just 16 to 17 years of age, whereas most young people leave their family home in their mid- to late 20s, and some young people leave home later. Many of these young people may also return to their family home for ongoing support or for help and assistance if they get into difficulties. There is also evidence that some young care leavers are likely to be living in unsuitable accommodation, move frequently and become homeless (A National Voice 2007; Stein and Morris 2010).

As suggested in Chapter 1, being in 'settled, safe accommodation' has to be considered in the context of connected and reinforcing pathways to adulthood: entering further and higher education or training, finding satisfying employment, and achieving good health and a positive sense of well-being – all pathways where there is evidence of care leavers being disadvantaged in comparison with other young people (Stein 2004; Stein and Munro 2008).

This chapter focuses upon how young people can be assisted with their accommodation.[1] A review of research studies suggests that for young people, being in 'settled, safe accommodation' involves a number of connected interventions (Stein and Morris 2010). These are:

---

1   This chapter and Chapters 5 and 6 draw upon and further develop material contained within Stein and Morris (2010).

- having a choice when to leave care
- being prepared
- having a choice of accommodation
- being and feeling safe
- being supported by workers, family, friends and mentors
- receiving financial assistance
- being involved in shaping services.

Having a choice when to leave care

For young people, having a choice of when to leave care and move on is very different from being expected to leave when they become 16, 17 or 18 years old (Morgan and Lindsay 2006). Consistent advice from Scottish young people who had left care to those leaving care in the future was: 'don't leave care too soon…don't believe it's as easy as people tell you, just be mature about it…don't run before you can walk…it's not as easy as you think' (Dixon and Stein 2005, p.159).

A survey of young people's views, by the Children's Rights Director for England, showed that at the time of leaving care, 41 per cent of young people did want to leave and 42 per cent didn't want to leave (other young people were not sure). However, when asked after leaving, if they left care at the right time, only a quarter thought that it was the right time, 45 per cent wished they had stayed in care longer and 17 per cent said that they should have left care earlier (Morgan and Lindsay 2012).

These views are also echoed by leaving care workers and personal advisers. In a survey of their views just over three-quarters thought that young people were leaving care at too young an age (A National Voice 2005). There is also evidence that foster carers are concerned that young people leave their care before they are ready (Sinclair *et al.* 2005). The only survey of housing workers' views (a sample of 82 housing workers from nine English regions) found that 80 per cent thought that young people left care too young (A National Voice 2005).

Young people's concerns about being expected to leave care before they were prepared and ready dates back to the 1970s (Stein 2011). But it was not until the introduction of the Children and Young Persons Act 2008 in April 2011 that legal provision was made to ensure that young people have a statutory review, to take into account their views before moving – so they do not leave care before they are ready (see Chapter 2). Also, from 2007 the then government introduced two pilot programmes, the Right2BCared4 Pilot Programme and the Staying Put 18+ Family Placement Programme, aimed at delaying young people's transitions from care until they were ready to leave. The main findings from the evaluation of Right2BCared4 (Munro *et al.* 2011) are summarised below (see Chapter 5 for a summary of Staying Put 18+).

EVALUATION OF THE RIGHT2BCARED4 PILOT PROGRAMME

INTRODUCTION

The Right2BCared4 pilot began in October 2007 in 11 local authorities and is based on the following principles:

- Young people should not be expected to leave care until they reach 18.

- They should have a greater say in the decision-making process preceding their exit from care.

- They should be properly prepared for living independently.

The evaluation carried out between January 2009 and October 2010 included: a mapping exercise and focus groups involving social workers, leaving care personal advisers, Independent Reviewing Officers (IROs) and other key professionals. It was undertaken in 11 pilot sites. In-depth work was then conducted in seven pilot authorities and two comparator (non-pilot) authorities.

KEY FINDINGS

- A higher proportion of those young people in the pilot authorities were looked after until they reached legal adulthood at 18 years of age compared with those from comparator authorities.

- In pilot areas IROs were more likely to be involved in pathway plan discussions and survey data revealed a high level of satisfaction with the support offered by IROs.

- There has been a cultural shift in professional attitudes concerning care planning for young people aged 16 years and over; professionals have become more proactive in encouraging young people to remain looked after until legal adulthood.

- Professionals identified that not all young people want to remain in care for longer. White British young women, especially parents, tend to leave care early. Those who have experienced multiple placement changes (often due to complex needs) are also likely to leave care early.

- It is important that packages of support are available to meet the needs of those who choose to move to independence.

- The majority of care leavers surveyed said that it was their choice to leave care.

- The figures reveal that a slightly higher percentage of those in the pilot authorities felt that they had had a choice about when they left compared with those from comparator authorities.

- Over half of those young people who moved into semi-independent or independent living arrangements were positive about their transitions. Around a quarter identified that the process of transition could have been improved and that moves had been rushed and abrupt.

- Young people generally felt involved in the pathway planning process. However, certain issues, including young people's relationships with their birth families and health needs, received minimal attention.

(Source: Adapted from Munro *et al.* 2011)

As detailed above, the evaluation highlights the role of the IRO including the importance of having someone who is seen as independent and impartial in order to discuss concerns about their relationship with, or the care provided by, their foster carers (Munro *et al.* 2011).

A report of children's views on IROs also shows their important role in ensuring children and young people's views are heard and that they have someone other than their social worker to ensure decisions are acted on (Ofsted 2011). Some of the pilot authorities sought to promote the use of advocacy services and this was highly rated by young people who used the service – although only a small number of advocates (11%) were involved in supporting young people with the pathway planning process (Munro *et al.* 2011). A scoping review of advocacy services for children and young people in England has shown the widespread use of these services but concluded 'there remains a postcode lottery for children attempting to access advocacy...in terms of availability, independence and accessibility' (Brady 2011, p.9).

Being prepared for leaving care

Being in safe and settled accommodation means young people being well prepared for leaving care. Research based on the views of young people shows that just under a quarter of care leavers thought that they had been well, or very well prepared for independent life after leaving care, and another 27 per cent that their preparation had been 'OK' – but this meant that nearly a half (49%) of young people thought that they had been 'prepared badly' or 'very badly' (Morgan and Lindsay 2012).

Pathway plans are an important part of both preparation and supporting young people after they leave care. Just over two-thirds (69%) of young people surveyed by the Children's Rights Director knew they had a pathway plan, just over a third had had their plan reviewed and just over a half said that their plans were being followed to some extent, although a quarter of young people reported that none of what was in their plan was being kept to (Morgan and Lindsay 2012).

In preparation for leaving care, young people want assistance with:

- practical skills, including budgeting, shopping, cooking and cleaning

- self-care skills, including personal hygiene, diet and health, sexual health, drugs and alcohol advice

- emotional and inter-personal skills, including personal well-being, and negotiating skills, such as managing encounters with officials, landlords and employers. (A National Voice 2005; Dixon and Stein 2005; Morgan and Lindsay 2006; Morgan and Lindsay 2012)

There is evidence that how well young people are prepared in these three main areas is significantly associated with how well young people cope after leaving care, practical skills and self-care skills having the most measurable effect. Young people who left care later and young women generally did better, the former emphasising the importance of being ready to leave care and the latter suggesting that more attention should be paid to the preparation skills of young men (Dixon and Stein 2005). Aspects of good practice in regard to preparation are detailed below.

GOOD PRACTICE IN PREPARATION

The following points are aspects of good practice identified in evaluations:

- assessment to identify young people's needs and how they will be met – this is an important part of the needs assessment and pathway planning process under the Children (Leaving Care) Act 2000 and the *Transitions Guidance*

- involving young people fully in the planning process – although not all young people feel that they are being involved enough in this critical process and there is evidence plans are not always updated (Morgan 2009a)

- case law (*Liverpool City Council v London Borough of Hillingdon*, 2009) suggests the 'wishes' of the young person are 'not determinative', and have to be considered in the context of 'assessed needs' and 'welfare', although this should not be seen as contrary to involving young people fully in the planning process

- providing ongoing support and opportunities for participation, involving discussion, negotiation and risk-taking

- the gradual learning of skills, in the context of a stable placement

- providing continuity of staff during care and at the time of leaving care

- carers being trained to assist care leavers.

(Source: Ofsted 2009; Stein and Morris 2010)

Preparation should also be responsive to ethnic diversity, culture and any disability the young person may have (Barn, Andrew and Mantovani 2005; Priestley *et al.* 2003; Zeira and Benbenishty 2011). Specialist leaving care schemes and programmes can assist carers with the development of skills training programmes, and by offering intensive compensatory help at the after-care stage (York Consulting Limited 2007).

Choice of accommodation

Local authorities are required to 'safeguard and promote the relevant child's welfare by...providing him with or maintaining him in suitable accommodation'. This is defined in the *Transitions Guidance* as accommodation:

- which, so far as reasonably practicable, is suitable for the child in the light of his needs, including his health needs

- in respect of which the responsible authority has satisfied itself as to the character and suitability of the landlord or other provider

- which complies with health and safety requirements related to rented accommodation

- in respect of which the responsible authority has, so far as is reasonably practicable, taken into account the child's:

  ◦ wishes and feelings

  ◦ educational, training or employment needs.

(Regulation 9(2) Care Leavers (England) Regulations 2010)

In deciding whether accommodation is suitable, local authorities must take into account the factors listed in Schedule 2 to the *Care Leavers (England) Regulations 2010* (and Schedule 6 of the *Care Planning, Placement and Case Review England Regulations 2010*). These are:

1. In respect of the accommodation, the

   - facilities and services provided

   - state of repair; safety

   - location

   - support

   - tenancy status, and

   - the financial commitments involved for the relevant child and their affordability.

2. In respect of the 'relevant child', their

   - views about the accommodation

   - understanding of their rights and responsibilities in relation to the accommodation, and

   - understanding of funding arrangements.

As discussed in Chapter 3, personal advisers have a pivotal role in respect of ensuring young people are in 'suitable accommodation' as part of the needs assessment and pathway planning process.

Strategic planning and partnerships are essential to the supply of 'suitable accommodation'. Under Section 27 of the Children Act 1989, a local authority can ask a range of other authorities, including a housing authority, to assist them in the exercise of their functions in relation to children in need and looked-after children (under Part 3 of the Act). The other authority must comply – to the extent that the request is compatible with their statutory duties. The main elements of successful strategic planning are identified by NCAS in *Journeys to Home: Care Leavers' Successful Transition to Independent Accommodation* (National Care Advisory Service 2009):

> Effective strategic work relies on a broad framework of funding streams and services. Formal relationships between children's services, housing agencies and other services need to underpin this framework to ensure that there is a high level commitment, effective communication, partnership working and joint planning across the authority. (p.9)

Young people also want a choice of accommodation matched to their needs. A National Voice surveyed 271 young people and found that over half of young people (55%) felt 'they had no real choice', and a third (32%) that the accommodation failed 'to meet their needs' (A National Voice 2005). Another survey of young people's views showed that just under a quarter of young people considered they were in the wrong accommodation for them, and just under 60 per cent thought their accommodation right for them. In the same survey, just under three-quarters of young people rated the standard of accommodation as either good or very good and one in ten rated their accommodation as bad or very bad (Morgan 2009a).

The range of first accommodation on leaving care identified in care leavers' studies includes:

- young people returning to their birth families

- young people staying on in foster care after they legally leave care, which may become 'supported lodgings'

- supported accommodation (supported lodgings, hostels, foyers (providing supported hostel accommodation), independent housing with floating support and trainer flats)

- independent housing (council and private tenancies)

- other settings (bed and breakfast accommodation, friends, custody) (Simon 2008; Wade and Dixon 2006).

A range of accommodation options is important in providing choice and this is likely to be influenced by local housing markets, as well as the contribution of the local authority acting as 'corporate parents' in securing access and supply for young people leaving care (National Care Advisory Service 2009; Rainer 2007).

Service providers have highlighted the different ways they have increased the supply of accommodation, including:

- developing joint protocols and working in partnership with housing authorities and associations

- providing training for the Corporate Parenting Board on the accommodation needs of care leavers, and involving young people in this process

- setting up 'corporate buy-ins' for looked-after young people, involving councillors; using 'supporting people' funding

- piloting 'staying put' foster placements (see Chapter 5)

- providing financial support for 'families and friends' care

- employing a housing officer to develop a range of provision in rural areas

- working regionally with other local authorities and housing providers.

Service providers have also drawn attention to the problems small local authorities have in providing a range of accommodation and in providing young people with extended support into adulthood (Stein and Morris 2010). However, the type of accommodation by itself tells us very little. What is equally relevant is whether young people like where they are living, whether they and their workers think that it meets their personal needs and whether the young person has the skills to cope with and manage their accommodation (Wade and Dixon 2006).

Being and feeling safe

Being and 'feeling safe' is a priority for young people (A National Voice 2005; Morgan and Lindsay 2006, National Care Advisory Service 2010a). 'A secure and safe place to live in' is the most important thing in making 'accommodation suitable' for young people (National Care Advisory Service 2010a). For young people 'being safe' means:

- A 'good location' where neighbours make an 'effort to be friendly' and living in a 'relatively crime-free area' (A National Voice 2005, pp.8–9).

- Not being housed in 'rough areas' or other temporary or transient accommodation, where there is often drug dealing, prostitution and where they could be the victims of break-ins (National Care Advisory Service 2010a).

- Having access to transport, education, training and employment, proximity to amenities, including shops, doctors and leisure facilities.

- Having support networks, including being close to friends and families, and not living in isolated areas – especially where there are poor and costly transport links (National Care Advisory Service 2010a).

There was also evidence of young people from black and minority ethnic groups being frightened of going out at night in predominantly 'rough' white areas (A National Voice 2005). Also important to young people in feeling safe was:

- The condition of the physical environment in which they were living: some young people had concerns about the physical state of the property they lived in, including cold and dampness, crumbling walls and infestations.

- Having access to services including: heating, hot water, electricity, telephone, television aerial, food preparation and storage 24 hours a day, floor coverings, furniture, furnishings and equipment (National Care Advisory Service 2010a).

- Feeling secure – having their own room and key, so they could lock it; lighting in communal areas; ensuring communal areas are lockable; having a mobile phone, to call for help, if needed; smoke detectors; and having a place where personal items can be locked away. Having health and safety checks – some young people had experience of poor security, faulty electrics and dangerous stairs (A National Voice 2005; National Care Advisory Service 2010a).

• Having safe play areas – young parents had been placed in accommodation without adequate play spaces and a lack of safety fencing.

An audit of leaving care services in London found that young people returning from 'out of authority placements', who are recognised as a highly vulnerable group, may have particular difficulties in accessing social or council accommodation, unless formal arrangements are in place (Vernon 2000). Service provider feedback included evidence that one local authority is proposing to offer all young people with complex needs returning from 'out of borough provision' a supported placement up to the age of 21 (Stein and Morris 2010). The feedback also recognised that young people who have been 'out of area' for a long time may wish to stay there – and it was essential to listen to young people's views about where they wish to live (Stein and Morris 2010).

Young disabled people may also miss out on access to mainstream housing as a result of inadequate planning between disability teams and leaving care services and, as a consequence, find that they are restricted to specialist disabled schemes (Morris 2002). For those young people who remained with their carer, being safe meant feeling 'physically and emotionally protected' – 'you're not going to come to any harm'. Being settled meant 'getting on well with your carers' (Stein and Morris 2010).

Practical and personal support

Young people want both practical and personal support in preparation for moving, at the time of moving on from care and when they have moved into their accommodation, including when they get into difficulties.

Evidence from young people aged between 16 and 23 shows that they want help in planning their move, including visiting the area before moving in, help in equipping their accommodation with the necessities, help in moving and help in setting up their accommodation, including decorating. They also want help in managing their accommodation, including budgeting, and domestic tasks – 'It is important that a carer helps you learn how to be independent.' Young people also recognised that carers need training and support in order to understand young people 'as a specific person' and recognise that young people need a 'chance to prove that we can live on our own' (Stein and Morris 2010).

In a NCAS survey of 93 young people's views of 'what is suitable accommodation?', 85 young people (92%) thought that it was 'very important' for young people to 'have contact details for support with 24 hours access' (National Care Advisory Service 2010a, p.17). In preparation for 'moving on', 90 per cent of the young people surveyed by NCAS were of the opinion that it was 'very important' they 'understand the nature of their rights and responsibilities set out in their tenancy agreement', and that 'all charges are detailed in their agreement' (p.19). Also, in preparation for moving they would like clear and easily understood information about their tenancy agreement and costs, including 'someone to read through the agreement…to ensure they understand all that is expected of them' (p.19). In setting up home young people would like assistance with transport for moving and their first big shop – and assistance with decorating and making their accommodation homely. Also, in the early days, young people welcome support with budgeting and help with benefits.

Young people are very aware of the importance of personal support, recognising that they have both social and emotional needs, including, from time to time being 'lonely and feeling depressed'. They want workers who they get on with and trust, do what they say they are going to do and who treat them with respect (Ofsted 2009). Generally, they would like support to be more accessible and available, including support outside of normal office hours, such as weekends and evenings (A National Voice 2005; Morgan and Lindsay 2006; National Care Advisory Service 2010a). Disabled young people would welcome more support in accessing social networks (National Foster Care Association 2000; Priestley et al. 2003). Young asylum seekers who are learning English may also have additional needs for personal support, especially in building social networks, as discussed in Chapter 10 (Chase, Knight and Statham 2008).

How are leaving care services responding to these support needs? The Children's Rights Director surveyed 135 young people who had recently left care and of these 70 per cent (94) rated the quality of the support they were getting after leaving care as 'good' or 'very good'. But this meant that for 20 per cent it was 'just about OK', for 6 per cent 'bad' and for 4 per cent 'very bad' (Morgan 2009a, 2009b). Similarly, about two-thirds of young people surveyed by A National Voice were 'happy' or 'very happy' with the after-care support they received and a similar proportion felt that when a problem arose help from leaving care services was useful (A National Voice 2005).

Two studies carried out following the introduction of the Children (Leaving Care) Act 2000 echo these positive findings (Simon 2008; Wade and Dixon 2006). The first follow-up study found that nearly all the young people (93%) had received support in achieving 'good' or 'fair' housing outcomes. At follow-up (12 to 15 months after leaving care), three-quarters were living in suitable accommodation and two-thirds of young people reported that they had been helped to look after their homes more effectively, and more than four in five young people reported that they had received help with finding somewhere to live (Wade and Dixon 2006).

The second study highlighted 'how young people's transitions were smoothed by both practical and emotional support' (Simon 2008, p.98). Ofsted's survey provides practice examples of the high levels of support being offered by leaving care teams, including out-of-hours support, a high-commitment 'can do' problem-solving approach, and assisting access to social and leisure facilities (Ofsted 2009). However, there is also evidence that mental health services are not responding to the high levels of need experienced by care leavers (Cameron *et al.* 2007; McAuley 2005).

Service providers have also highlighted the lack of resources in meeting the needs of young people with more challenging emotional and behavioural needs. Their suggestions and practice examples include: developing a regional approach to commissioning services by grouping together commissioning with neighbouring local authorities providing intensive support (ongoing and out-of-hours); giving young people the opportunity to return to foster and residential care; working jointly with adult services on transitions; and having a range of supported accommodation (lodgings; intensive residential support projects; trainer/transitional flats) (Stein and Morris 2010).

Social networks: support from families, friends and former carers

Young people can also benefit from informal support from families, former carers and friends. Having a 'sense of family' is symbolically important to care leavers, as it is to other young people – even though they recognise that it was often their families who failed them, and that for many young people poor family relationships ruled out a return home (Sinclair *et al.* 2005). The limited available research evidence on this topic shows that:

- For some young people, over time, there can be increased contact and reconciliation between young people and their parents (Wade 2008).

- Parents and friends can offer help when young people get into difficulties with their accommodation as well as practical help, including help with money and company, especially where young people have settled in the same neighbourhood (Simon 2008).

- Young people most often cited 'mothers' as the person they would turn to if in need of help – brothers and sisters, aunts, nieces and nephews, and grandparents were also identified (Dixon and Stein 2005; Wade 2008).

- Some young people were able to sustain a relationship with their foster carers, or have good relationships with their partner's family (Sinclair *et al.* 2005).

- There are examples of formalising attachments with foster carers – foster carers being paid a retainer while a young person was at university and then full-board when they returned (Sinclair *et al.* 2005).

The experience of living in care may also inhibit or prevent young people's social networks. Feeling different because of being in care and frequent change of placements could result in transitory or very weak friendships, especially at school or in the local neighbourhood, contributing to a lack of social support at the time of leaving care. Their vulnerability at this time may also be increased by low self-esteem and lack of autonomy (Ridge and Millar 2000).

However, the renewal of family relationships could also be a mixed blessing – sometimes helpful, other times disappointing as past difficulties resurfaced. Some young people leaving foster care are unable to psychologically distance themselves from the traumas they have suffered at the hands of their birth families – they are psychologically held back from being able to move on from care and find satisfaction with their lives after care (McAuley 2005; Sinclair *et al.* 2005). However, as Blakeslee (2011) has argued, the contribution of formal and informal social networks to outcomes during transition has not been rigorously explored – although 'the social network functions provided through stable and supportive relationships may be critically important during youth transitions from foster care' (p.2).

Mentoring schemes

Mentoring schemes may also offer support to young people leaving care (Ahrens *et al.* 2008; Clayden and Stein 2005; McBriar, Noade and Ringland 2001). They can be seen as occupying a space between formal or professional support and the informal support by families or friends, in assisting care leavers during their journey to adulthood. Research on resilience has given support to mentoring by highlighting the importance of a caring and consistent adult in the lives of vulnerable young people to help them overcome a range of problems (Stein 2005). Young people valued the advice they received from mentors during their transition to independence. They thought that mentoring had helped them with: important practical advice, particularly in relation to maintaining their accommodation; education and finding work; and relationship problems, building their confidence and improving their emotional well-being. The mentor's views on the impact of mentoring generally reflected the young people's views (Clayden and Stein 2005).

Financial support

The *Transitions Guidance* makes it clear that the 'financial arrangements' which are essential to young people being able to meet and sustain their accommodation costs should be addressed in the needs assessment and content of the pathway plans (see Appendix 1, 7: Financial Arrangements)

Understandably, young people are acutely aware of the importance of financial support – including being in education, employment and training – in sustaining their accommodation (Morgan 2009a; Morgan and Lindsay 2006). There is evidence that disadvantaged young people, including those leaving care, recognise that they are held back by a lack of qualifications (Calder and Cope 2003). Some young people also regard expectations as too low (Jackson and Sachdev 2001). Follow-up research carried out since the introduction of the Children (Leaving Care) Act 2000 shows:

- Young people not completing post-16 further education courses, some 12 to 15 months after leaving care.

- The 'mediating contribution' of 'good' housing outcomes to 'good' career outcomes and mental well-being.

- The importance of specific careers advice.

- The contribution of leaving care later (age 18 or over) to positive career outcomes.

- Young people who leave care younger and those who have mental health, emotional or behavioural difficulties are more than twice as likely to have poor career outcomes. (Wade and Dixon 2006)

As regards financial support received under the Children (Leaving Care) Act 2000, there is evidence from three surveys of considerable variation in the amounts of leaving care grants (including financial assistance to set up home, and help with education and employment) received by young people (A National Voice 2005; Care Leavers' Foundation 2009; Morgan and Lindsay 2012).

The 2005 A National Voice survey of 271 young people showed that the amount received in the setting-up-home grant varied from nothing (29% of young people) to £2000 or more (just 1% of young people). Of the 231 leaving care workers/personal advisers surveyed, 84 per cent thought that the grant should be increased. Sixty-eight per cent of the 80 housing workers surveyed also thought that the grant should be higher (A National Voice 2005). The Care Leavers' Foundation survey calculated that young people needed £2500 for the most basic furnishings and essentials to enable them to live independently – but only one out of 150 local authorities surveyed provided this sum (Care Leavers' Foundation 2009).

Research based on young people's views carried out by the Children's Rights Director for England showed that under a third of young people (29%) thought that they were 'given enough, or nearly enough' financial help with daily living expenses, and a quarter viewed the help given as 'nowhere near enough' (Morgan and Lindsay 2012). In the same survey, over half (56%) were getting some financial help towards their education or training, but only 19 per cent felt that it 'was enough' or 'nearly enough' and 16 per cent said it was 'nowhere near enough' (Morgan and Lindsay 2012).

In a policy paper, NCAS have highlighted the problems for care leavers being expected to claim benefits at 18 years of age, including managing their own income and household, and claiming housing benefit to part-fund continuing placements with former foster carers (National Care Advisory Service 2010b). They argue that this distinguishes them from most of their peers who remain at home and do not claim benefits, especially if they are in further education. They suggest that the current dual system of support (benefits and local authority payments) can result in: inconsistencies in support; disincentives to move into education, training and employment; problems for some vulnerable young people in maintaining their housing; and young people being uncomfortable when the status of the former carer they continue to live with changes to a 'landlord'. They propose that local authorities as 'corporate parents' should provide financial support for care leavers in further education (as parents do) until they reach 21 years of age (National Care Advisory Service 2010b).

Being involved in decisions

Young people want to be involved in decisions both about their individual care – including their accommodation needs – and the services that they receive. As regards the former, the evidence presented above suggests that there is variation in practice at different stages of the process. Although many young people feel involved, not all think that they have a real choice when they leave care, or are involved in their assessment and pathway planning, or feel that they have a choice of 'suitable accommodation' and support matched to their needs (A National Voice 2005; Morgan and Lindsay 2006; National Care Advisory Service 2010a). There is evidence that advocacy services may assist young people, including with accommodation issues, although not all service-level agreements include young people aged over 18 (Ofsted 2009; Stein 2009b).

There is evidence of young people being involved in shaping the services they receive. This includes participation in supported lodgings and fostering panels, corporate parenting panels, local authority youth parliaments and children in care panels, and various strategy groups, including those related to accommodation and homelessness (National Care Advisory Service 2009; Ofsted 2009). They are also involved in training and recruiting staff, meetings and training with councillors and senior staff, as 'corporate parents', and assisting other looked-after young people as peer mentors. Some young people were also playing an active role in the work of A National Voice and NCAS.

Summary points

The studies discussed in this chapter, which include the views of young people about being in 'settled, safe accommodation', suggest that it can be viewed as part of a process involving a number of different stages:

- Having a choice when to leave care placements – not just being expected to leave at 16 or 17 years of age. There is evidence that professionals have become more proactive in encouraging young people to remain in care longer. The requirement of a statutory review and the contribution of IROs and advocacy services should also contribute to young people leaving care when they feel prepared and ready to leave.

- Being well prepared in practical, self-care and emotional and inter-personal skills and feeling ready to move on. Evaluations of good practice highlight the importance of assessment, involving young people fully, providing ongoing support and opportunities for risk taking, the gradual learning of skills, continuity and carers being trained to assist young people.

- Having a good choice of accommodation matched to their assessed needs and taking into account any additional needs they may have.

- Being in a safe neighbourhood in accommodation in good physical condition and close to amenities, including shops, educational and leisure facilities.

- Being well supported – by leaving care workers, by mentors and by building on positive social networks, including support by family and friends.

- Being in education, employment or training, having an income or receiving adequate financial assistance.

Chapter 5

Carers and Accommodation

> She was always there for me…if I had a problem I could tell her about it and she would help me deal with it…I could talk about my problems, I was loved.

This chapter explores how carers, including foster carers, residential carers, kinship carers and birth families, can assist young people with their accommodation. A central theme of this book is that how young people fare in respect of their main pathways to adulthood, including accommodation, is in part connected to the quality of care they receive: carers providing stable high-quality placements provide the emotional foundations for the present and future well-being of young people (Sinclair *et al.* 2007). Peer research on the views of 250 young people identified 'the best things about care' as: feeling emotionally secure and supported by their carers; feeling safe; having opportunities for fun and enjoyment; having opportunities for self-development; having financial and material support; and having new friendships, bonds and social skills (Miller and Sweetman 2007). For most young people, their families provide them with their platform, or launch pad, to adulthood – how can carers assist young people with this process?

Foster care: extended placements and supported lodgings

Foster carers may provide young people with the opportunity of 'staying put' in extended placements or 'stand-alone' supported lodgings. There are also supported lodging schemes aimed at young people experiencing homelessness. A benchmarking survey of 62 supported lodging schemes carried out in 2011 showed that the majority had been in place for at least two years and a third had been running for over ten years. Most of the schemes were in-house local authority schemes run by the fostering or leaving care teams and varied from one to five hosts or carers to schemes with over 50 carers – although the majority work with fewer than 20 young people. Most of the young people stayed between one and two years (Fostering Network 2011).

Extended placements

Building on the foundations of good-quality care, foster carers can assist young people with their accommodation by giving them the opportunity to remain with their carers beyond the age of 18, where they are settled and want to stay. This means that young people will be able to leave care gradually, when they are prepared and ready to leave – more akin to the journey made by other young people. Research studies show that this process, as distinct from the accelerated and compressed transitions made by many care leavers, is associated with better outcomes (Courtney, Lee and Perez 2011; Stein 2004) Government recognition of these research findings led in 2008 to the introduction of the Staying Put 18+ Family Placement Pilot Programme in 11 English local authorities (see below).

EVALUATION OF THE STAYING PUT 18+ FAMILY PLACEMENT PILOT PROGRAMME

The Staying Put 18+ Family Placement Pilot Programme was introduced in 11 local authorities in July 2008, giving young people who have 'established familial relationships' the opportunity to remain with their foster carers up to the age of 21. The evaluation was carried out between 2009 and 2011 and included a mapping exercise, and interviews with managers in the 11 pilot authorities, followed by peer research interviews with young people (21 staying put; 11 who did not); interviews with their carers and personal advisers; and collection of data to facilitate estimation of costs of rolling out the programme.

KEY FINDINGS: THE BENEFITS OF 'STAYING PUT'

• Empowers young people and gives them greater control of the timing of their transition from care to adulthood, rather than them feeling that they are being 'kicked out' of the system.

- Young people are not penalised by virtue of their care status; they are offered the opportunity to experience transitions that are more akin to those experienced by their peers in the general population.

- Allows young people to remain in a nurturing family environment where they can mature and develop, prepare for independence and receive support.

- Those in the staying put group were more likely to sustain their engagement in education, employment and training compared with those who did not: they were more that twice as likely to be in full-time education at 19; more likely to be in full-time training and employment at 19 and far less likely not to be in education, employment and training than those who did not stay put.

- A key factor influencing both foster carer's decisions to extend placements and young people's willingness to stay put was the quality of those relationships and the extent to which attachments had been established. This highlights the importance of effective care planning and matching.

- In-depth qualitative data on a small sample of young people also revealed that those who did not stay put were more likely to experience complex transition pathways and housing instability after they left care.

THE CHALLENGES

- In most pilot authorities young people had to have an 'established familial relationship' and be in EET (education, employment or training), potentially excluding more vulnerable young people including late entrants to care, those with a history of instability, those with emotional and behavioural difficulties, and those not in EET.

- Not all young people are willing and able to stay put and will need ongoing support services into adulthood.

(Source: Adapted from Munro *et al.* 2012)

The main objectives of the 'Staying Put' pilot were: to enable young people to build on and nurture their attachments to their foster carers, so that they can move to independence at their own pace and be supported to make the transition to adulthood in a more gradual way just like other people who can rely on their families for this support; provide the stability necessary for young people to achieve in education, training and employment; and give weight to young people's views about the timing of moves to greater independence from their final care placement.

An evaluation of a foster care scheme for young people remaining with their foster carers up to 21 years of age carried out in Northern Ireland described their role as helping young people mature and become independent (McCrea 2008). The evaluation showed that foster carers need the attitudes, skills and abilities to assist young people on a range of fronts including:

- motivation and encouragement with education, training and employment and helping them find suitable work

- making decisions about their future

- emotional support, including dealing with past issues, help with relationships, social networks and friendships

- inter-personal skills, self-esteem and boundary setting and decision-making

- finances to support young people and maintain their interests, hobbies and keep up to date with current fashion

- independence skills such as managing and running a home, budgeting and debt management and help with preparation towards independent living

- supporting young people's contact with their birth parent(s)

- opportunities for peer support.

The scheme evaluation shows that young people, in the main, thought that their foster carers were successful in meeting their needs in these respects and in recognising the changing 'parenting role' with young adults. As regards 'interventions' to support their role, the foster carers welcomed the support they received but wanted:

- more clarification of the separate roles and responsibilities of personal advisers, social workers and carers
- more training on specific issues related to their roles (as identified above)
- opportunities for peer support meetings
- increased financial support, in recognition of the costs associated with supporting young people in this age group with regard to education, employment and training, and especially lifestyle issues.

In Northern Ireland nearly 25 per cent of young people aged 16 plus in care are in extended placements provided by foster and kinship carers (Fostering Network 2011). The aim of the GEM programme is for young people to continue in placements after they reach the age of 18 years (see below).

GOING THE EXTRA MILE SUPPORTED LODGING SCHEME

The Going the Extra Mile scheme (GEM) is offered as an option as part of the pathway planning process for care leavers in Northern Ireland. Nearly a quarter of young people aged 16 or over in care are in GEM schemes and this is rising annually. £1.1m over three years has been ring-fenced exclusively from the social services budget for the GEM scheme on a 'spend to save' basis. The model is flexible, focuses on maintaining relationships and seeks to ensure that the young people have a home to come back to – whether they are on a gap year, away at university or leave to live independently, but then want to return to the carer's home because it is not working out for them.

AIMS OF THE SCHEME

- To provide continuity and stability of placements.
- Better support whilst in education, employment or training.
- Normalisation of the pathway out of care.
- Valuing the contribution of carers, many of whom are deeply committed to the young people in their care.
- Giving young people choice.

KEY ASPECTS OF THE SCHEME

- GEM continues to pay foster carers their allowance, up to a maximum of £152 a week, which is the most that can be paid for 16–17 year olds.

- Anyone who is in foster care, or who comes into it aged 16 or over, is offered the option of the scheme. It provides an opportunity for young people to come back two or three times or more if that's what's needed.

- Being in education, employment or training, very broadly defined, is a prerequisite for eligibility.

- Carers have to be open to the possibility of being a GEM carer.

- Financial provision is on a sliding scale.

- What young people and carers need in terms of support is monitored through the pathway plan; and social workers regularly assess how the placement is going.

BENEFITS OF THE SCHEME

- Young people are better prepared and have a gradual journey to adulthood.

- Investing in the future welfare of young people after they leave care.

- Young people have better engagement in EET.

- Carers are recognised as being 'good parents'.

CHALLENGES FOR THE SCHEME

- Sustainability and affording growth.

- The cap on allowances payable to foster carers.

- Interface with adult disability.

- Training and support of carers.

- Limitations for young people in specialised care placements.

(Source: Adapted from Fostering Network 2011)

Schofield's study (2002) is one of the very few which attempts to identify the qualities of foster carers, as well as the 'interventions' needed that may contribute to positive outcomes. Drawing on the accounts of 40 young adults from care, Schofield proposes a 'psychosocial model of long-term foster care'. The study identifies five main domains: to love – promoting felt security; to act – promoting self-efficacy; to think – promoting resolution of loss and trauma and developing reflective functions; to belong – promoting family membership in childhood and adult life; and to hope – promoting resilience (see Chapter 12).

Stand-alone supported lodgings

As well as extended placements (which are also sometimes referred to as 'Foster Care Conversions'), young people may be placed in stand-alone supported lodging provision. These may have been specifically developed for care leavers or open to other groups of vulnerable young people. However, if a 16 or 17 year old looked-after young person is placed in supported lodgings it is likely to meet the definition of a fostering placement (National Care Advisory Service 2009).

There are two main types of stand-alone provision. First, short-term emergency lodgings which are often provided in response to a crisis, for example, a breakdown of a foster care or children's home placement. In this context an emergency placement may prevent the young person becoming homeless or ending up in unsatisfactory accommodation, as exemplified by the Safe and Sound Homes (SASH) project (outlined below). It can also provide an opportunity for the worker and young person to explore future options.

SAFE AND SOUND HOMES

Safe and Sound Homes (SASH) works in four local authority areas and runs the following schemes:

- Nightstop – short-term emergency accommodation in the homes of volunteer hosts.

- Crashpad – a longer-term version of Nightstop.

- Supported Lodgings – accommodation with hosts/carers for up to two years.

Young people can access Nightstop then can continue on the accommodation pathway into Crashpad and ultimately into Supported Lodgings. Crashpad is used as the assessment point for young people to then move into Supported Lodgings. SASH has hosts/carers across Yorkshire. Supported Lodgings provide an environment where young people's behaviour can be moulded and modified to better prepare them for adult life.

The values that the SASH team work towards when working with young people are: being respectful; helping others; being honest and conscientious; being fair, and working relationships with young people being adult to adult.

Young people are encouraged to see engagement in the scheme as the beginning of the end of some of their problems and the start of something new. Hosts/carers are also trained to understand and support young people's aspirations.

(Source: Adapted from Fostering Network 2011)

The second option is longer-term supported lodgings. These can be used to support young people during their journey from care to adulthood and closely resemble the contribution of extended placements described above, in terms of the carer's skills and the assistance given to young people. There is also evidence that they can make a very positive contribution to the lives of young people in respect of maintaining their accommodation, avoiding eviction, continuing in education and work and participating in social activities, although they may not be suitable for young people with very complex needs who are unable to relate to their carers and not engaged in education, employment or training (Fostering Network 2011).

A survey of supported lodging schemes in England shows that between 10 and 25 per cent of young people leaving care in any one year have lived in supported lodgings (including emergency and longer-term) and that the quality and provision is very patchy – it is not always available to young people as part of the range of housing options in different local authorities (Fostering Network 2011). However as the Fostering Network suggests:

> Local authorities should recognise the flexibility of supported lodgings
> as a housing option for young people...that can fulfil a range of

functions to support young people's transitions to independence. For example:

- Short term, quick access to Nightstop or Supported Lodgings for use as quality emergency accommodation or to provide 'time out' to support homelessness prevention through family reconciliation.

- Longer term Supported Lodgings for young people needing settled supported accommodation as part of their transition towards independent living (including young people leaving care, 16 and 17 year olds accommodated under section 20 of the Children Act 1989 and other young people needing accommodation because of homelessness).

- Low level Supported Lodgings for young people with few support needs but who need a safe, affordable place to live. (Fostering Network 2011, p.28)

Foster care: providing ongoing support

Another way in which foster carers may assist young people with their accommodation is through providing ongoing support after young people have left their care. The evidence suggests that:

- Such contact is common at first but drops off sharply over time.

- It is generally very positive for young people and may reduce social isolation.

- It can support young people in their life and social skills – both of which may help young people remain in their accommodation.

- It is unlikely to be able to help young people when they face major difficulties in their lives.

- As an 'intervention' it is invisible, in that it takes place informally, outside of the pathway planning process and without financial support. (Sinclair *et al.* 2005; Wade 2008)

Jackson and Thomas (2001) provide the example of a 'pro-teen fostering' project. This made provision for young people, who found it too difficult to cope alone, to return to their foster placement until they felt they were prepared and ready to be 're-launched'. The project also provided the foster carers with additional and flexible financial support to maintain ongoing contact with the young people they cared for.

Parents and carers are of the view that young people should be able to return to care when things don't work out for them – 'the door is open...as with young people who leave home'. 'Care leavers would benefit from similar support provided by parents...this usually lasts for many years, if not for a lifetime in terms of emotional support...ideally this would be the same person they had developed a relationship with during their time in care'. They believed the carer should meet up with the young people they cared for on a regular basis to ensure they are well. They also thought that there is a need for more specialist provision within the area where young people live, so they do not have to be placed in 'out of authority' placements (Stein and Morris 2010).

Residential workers

There is little research on the contribution of residential workers in assisting young people with their accommodation on leaving care (Bostock *et al.* 2009). However, research into the outcomes of a social-pedagogical approach in residential care in Germany showed that positive gains made while in care – in education, life management, reduced offending, personality development and social relations – had been maintained for a majority of young people four to five years after leaving care (Stein and Munro 2008).

Social pedagogy represents a different approach to the practice of residential work in England, including different training and skills. Cameron *et al.* (2011) see it as 'an educational approach to social issues. Its breadth can be seen in its concern for the whole person as emotional, thinking and physical beings, promoting their active engagement in decisions about their own lives and as members of society' (p.8). Research comparing English, German and Danish children's homes showed that those in Germany and Denmark employing social pedagogues considered it an important part of their role to help young people find suitable accommodation (Petrie *et al.* 2006). Also, in Denmark and Spain young people may remain in residential care beyond 18 years of age and receive support into adulthood (Höjer *et al.* 2008).

A study evaluating the social pedagogy pilot programme in children's homes in England found that there were no significant differences in behavioural, emotional or educational outcomes, or in the quality of family contact between children and young people living in the pilot or comparison homes after seven months follow-up – homes that employed social pedagogues did no better or worse than those which did not, and disruptions were as likely to occur in the pilot homes as in the comparison group. Both good-quality care and 'insensitive practices' were found in both pilot and comparative homes (Berridge *et al.* 2011).

There is evidence from England of young people keeping in touch with residential workers after they leave children's homes. Keeping in touch with former carers brings benefits to young people and is an unacknowledged and unsupported 'intervention' (Wade 2008).

Social networks: kinship care

Based on the 2001 Census data, it is estimated that the number of children in formal and informal kinship care in England was 142,376, and of these 6870 were looked-after children but the great majority, 95 per cent (136,497), were living in informal kinship care (Nandy and Selwyn 2011). The Census data also showed that older children, particularly those aged between 15 and 17 were most likely to be living with their kin. Children and young people of minority ethnicity were over-represented among the kinship care population and this was particularly pronounced for those of Black African origin.

The three distinct groups of kinship carers were grandparents, siblings and other relatives, including aunts, uncles and cousins. Between one-fifth and a half of children living with kin were living with a sibling. There is also evidence that children living with kin experience high levels of poverty, which is associated with poor health, social development and educational attainment, and many kinship families are headed by a lone female carer, most often a grandmother (Nandy and Selwyn 2011).

Research studies on looked-after children in kinship care in England have, in the main, focused on younger children and as a consequence very little attention has been given to transitions from care to adulthood from such placements, including the adult outcomes of former kinship care children (Iglehart 2004; Stein 2009b). For example, in Farmer and Moyers' study of 142 young people in kinship care, 85 per cent were under 15 years at selection, and the focus of the study – including the 21 young people who were aged 15 and older (15%) – was on young people under 18 years before moving on to live independently. In respect of 'plans for children', the aim in 93 per cent of these kinship care placements was to provide a 'long-term home' – and for none of the older young people, was 'preparation for independence' planned (Farmer and Moyers 2008).

Only one English study, by Broad *et al.* (2001), casts light on the contribution of kinship carers that may be seen as helping young people feel safe and settled in accommodation. From the viewpoint of young people, kinship care was seen as very positive. It made them:

- feel loved, valued and cared for, especially after being in care or by not going into care

- feel safe from harm and threatening behaviour in care

- feel they are listened to

- sustain a sense of who they are, through contact with family, siblings and friends

- feel that they belong and feel settled, especially in not being moved around.

The potential contribution of kinship care in providing young people with 'settled, safe accommodation' is under-developed – currently only about 12 per cent of looked-after children, of all ages, are placed with 'family and friends' in England (Farmer and Moyers 2008). This contrasts sharply with Spain where 80 per cent of foster care placements are provided by kinship carers. Research shows that most young people find this a very positive experience, one that gives them stability and lays the career foundations for adulthood, the process of transition being similar to young people leaving foster care in Spain (Del Valle *et al.* 2011).

There is also evidence that young people identify a wide range of family members in their kinship network who they regard as their 'closest family', including siblings, aunts and uncles, and grandparents. Yet both social workers and leaving care workers are not good at identifying them or involving them in leaving care planning (Wade 2008). Research carried out in Australia on care planning showed that young people living in relative and kinship care saw themselves as less involved in the planning process than were their carers (McDowell 2011): it was observed that 'while caseworkers may be reluctant to intrude on a "family" context in kinship care, the need of these young people for support in many areas should not be overlooked' (p.viii).

Birth families

As discussed in Chapter 4 birth family relationships can be a mixed blessing. Where they are positive they can provide both practical and emotional support to young people, including assistance with accommodation and help when they may get into difficulties (Marsh and Peel 1999; Simon 2008).

Research into the views of birth parents shows that they would like to be more involved in the plans when young people leave care (Stein and Morris 2010). However, as discussed earlier (see p.56), some young people have very negative experiences within their birth families and this casts a long shadow on their lives after they leave care.

In this context, assessment of birth parents' attitudes, skills and abilities – and the 'interventions' needed in supporting parents – in meeting young people's accommodation needs will be critical to the pathway planning process. Using family group conferences as part of the pathway planning process may be an effective way of identifying the strengths and weaknesses of family and social networks in assisting young people during their transition to adulthood (Marsh and Peel 1999).

Summary points

- Young people who remain in foster care until they are prepared and ready to leave can be assisted to make a better transition to adulthood than those who leave care early.

- Young people may also be assisted by supported lodging schemes. These may provide both short- and longer-term options for young people. 'Staying put' options are less likely to be available to young people who are not in education, employment or training, or who have more complex needs.

- Both foster and residential carers do provide ongoing support to young people who have left their care, although this receives little formal recognition in terms of pathway planning.

- There is very little research on young people leaving care either by moving into, or moving on from, kinship care. The limited evidence does suggest that it is seen as very positive by young people. Its potential should, therefore, be further explored.

- Positive birth family relationships can provide young people with both practical and emotional support but negative relationships can be very damaging for young people.

- Young people also identify a wide range of family members beyond their birth families who they see as their 'closest family' and who could also be seen as a potential source of support. But, again, there is little evidence of their involvement in the pathway planning process.

- Good-quality assessments and using family group conferences as part of pathway planning is the key to identifying supportive family and social networks.

Chapter 6

Homelessness, Housing Outcomes and Leaving Care Services

> I was in a bed-sit on my own… I couldn't handle it, being on my own, being lonely, no family behind me, no friends. I was stopping in at home being bored… I got into financial difficulties and was evicted.

It is estimated that just under 80,000 young people in the general population experience homelessness across the United Kingdom, including young people who are statutorily accepted as homeless, young people using supported housing services (defined as homeless by professionals) and rough sleepers (Quilgars, Fitzpatrick and Pleace 2011). The numbers of young people formally accepted as statutorily homeless in England has shown a steady decrease over recent years in England, partly as a result of preventative measures including family mediation or supporting young people to manage a tenancy.

There are also official data showing an improvement in the numbers of care leavers in 'suitable accommodation' between 2005 and 2011, although there are still variations between local authorities and regions: between 2009 and 2011, on average, 90 per cent of young people were in 'suitable accommodation', but during this period only seven local authorities were housing all their care leavers in suitable accommodation (Department for Education 2011a; Stein and Morris 2010).

However, the policy context under the coalition government is changing and is likely to have a disproportionate impact upon vulnerable young people through: youth unemployment; cuts in spending on non-statutory youth services; changes to the Local Housing Allowance; an extension of the Single Room Rent Rate to include those under the age of 35 (instead of 25); the abolition of the Educational Maintenance

Allowance; and the ending of ring-fencing of Supporting People funding.

This chapter explores four questions: first, what is the legal and policy framework for preventing homelessness among young people leaving care? Second, what is the relationship between housing outcomes and homelessness? Third, which groups of care leavers are most vulnerable to poor housing outcomes? Fourth, how effective are leaving care services in improving accommodation outcomes?

The legal framework for preventing homelessness

The vulnerability of care leavers to homelessness is recognised in housing legislation. Care leavers, aged 18–20, and those aged 21 or over who are vulnerable, as a result of having been looked after, accommodated or fostered, are identified as a 'priority need group' under Part 7 of the Housing Act 1996. However, as the *Transitions Guidance* makes clear:

> There should be no expectation that care leavers will be treated as 'homeless' when their care placement comes to an end, in order to place the housing authority under an obligation to secure accommodation under Part 7 of the 1996 Act. (p.56)

The Homelessness Act 2002 places a duty on Housing and Social Services Departments to develop joint strategies to prevent homelessness among vulnerable groups, including care leavers.

In May 2009, the House of Lords made a landmark judgment in the case of *R (G) v London Borough of Southwark*. The Lords ruled that the primary duty to a homeless 16 or 17 year old is under the Children Act 1989: the ongoing duty to accommodate and support that young person will normally fall to the children's services authority. The judgment made it clear that children's services cannot avoid their duty to accommodate a homeless 16 or 17 year old under Section 20 of the Children Act 1989 by claiming they were providing assistance by using their powers under Section 17 of the Act, or by helping the young person to get accommodation through homelessness legislation. Young people who are accommodated under Section 20 are 'looked-after children' who will in due course become entitled to services under the Children (Leaving Care) Act 2000. In other words they will be entitled to the same full range of support under the Act as other eligible young people.

In April 2010 (in response to *R (G) v London Borough of Southwark* the government issued guidance to children's services and local housing authorities to secure or provide accommodation for homeless 16 and 17 year old young people (Department for Children, Schools and Families and Communities and Local Government 2010). The main provisions include:

- Preventing homelessness among 16 and 17 year olds through work with families such as family mediation and family group conferences.

- Children's services are the lead agency with regard to assessing and meeting the needs of 16 and 17 year olds who seek help because of homelessness, however, 'integrated services can assist in the delivery of a seamless, child-centred response' (p.5).

- Where an initial referral or approach has been made to housing services under Part 7 of the 1996 Housing Act (including where interim accommodation has been provided under the Act), there should be an immediate referral to children's services for an assessment 'if the young person may be homeless or may be likely to become homeless within 28 days' (p.4).

- Where a 16 or 17 year old has 'nowhere to stay that night, then children's services must secure suitable emergency accommodation for them...they will become looked after (under Section 20(1)) whilst their needs for continuing accommodation and support are further assessed' (p.6).

- Bed-and-breakfast accommodation is not considered suitable accommodation for 16 and 17 year olds even on an emergency basis (p.60).

- Children's services 'should undertake and complete an initial assessment as soon as possible and no later than the ten days set out in the Framework for the Assessment of Children in Need and their families' (p.4) and 'where children's services have accepted that they have a duty under Section 20 to provide accommodation and the 16 and 17 year old has accepted the accommodation, the young person will not be homeless' (pp.4–5).

- Assessment, support and accommodation services should take into account young peoples' relationships as well as any dependent children and, where appropriate, support them to build a positive family life (p.3).

- Children's services should also consider during the assessment process 'whether they should provide services under Section 17 of the 1989 Act (The Children Act 1989), which could include financial support under Section 17(6) to sustain any plan for the young person to live with members of their family' (p.9).

- Where children's services decide they do not have a duty to provide accommodation, or a 16 or 17 year old refuses accommodation (under Section 20 of the 1989 Act), housing services need to consider whether any duty is owed under Part 7 of the 1966 Housing Act. If they are accommodated under Part 7 of the 1966 Act, 'children's services should work closely with housing services to ensure he or she does not become homeless intentionally in the future, for example, as a result of accruing rent arrears or being evicted due to bad behaviour' (p.15).

- 'It is essential that services for homeless 16 and 17 year olds are underpinned by written joint protocols which set out clear, practical arrangements for providing services that are centred on the young people and their families and prevent young people from being passed from pillar to post' (p.17).

Homelessness and housing outcomes

Research studies show that about one-third of young people experience homelessness at some stage between 6 and 24 months after leaving care (Dixon and Stein 2005; Wade and Dixon 2006). The pattern in these follow-up studies was for these young people to move in and out of homelessness and there was not necessarily a connection between single episodes of homelessness and final housing outcomes.

In these studies homelessness had involved young people staying – or more likely 'kipping on the floor or the sofa' – with family or friends to prevent them sleeping rough, stopping at homeless hostels or refuges, sleeping rough or spending short periods in bed-and-breakfast accommodation. The provision of more 'emergency accommodation' and better planning could prevent some of these episodes (National Care Advisory Service 2009; Ofsted 2009), as exemplified by the Young People's Housing Hub Service (see below). Opportunities for young people to return to foster care placements could also be considered (Jackson and Thomas 2001).

THE YOUNG PEOPLE'S HOUSING HUB SERVICE: MEETING THE NEEDS OF YOUNG PEOPLE IN HOUSING NEED OR CRISIS

Hull City Council has introduced a Young People's Housing Hub Service, as part of its Young People's Support Service (YPSS), to assist young people, including care leavers, who are in housing need or crisis.

The Hub service has a dedicated team including housing, family mediation and youth offending staff – providing a single port of call. The Hub aims to minimise homelessness and the numbers of young people accepted as statutory homeless. Its services include: emergency and temporary accommodation; mediation (between young people and family, carers, housing providers); pre-tenancy training (to assist young people with the skills to maintain their tenancy); supported lodgings which provide 54 placements enabling young people to live with a family to prepare them for independent living; and advice to all young people up to 25 years of age about a range of housing options and how to access them.

The Hub service has contributed to 'a sustained decrease' in the numbers of care leavers becoming homeless, as well as reductions in the use of bed-and-breakfast accommodation. The YPSS, of which the Hub is part, aims to help young people learn the skills they need for independent living – contributing to the prevention of homelessness.

An independent evaluation of the YPSS found that: 75 per cent of young people were happy with the support they had received in finding accommodation; most of the young people felt that they had been given enough choice in terms of location and type of accommodation; and they valued the help and advice they had been given. During the first three-quarters of 2009–2010, 100 per cent of young people were returned as being in 'suitable accommodation'.

(Source: practice example in Stein and Morris 2010)

There is evidence that the proportion of rough sleepers with a care background has fallen from 17 per cent in 2001–2002, to 7 per cent in 2007–2008. As Savage observes, 'The findings do suggest an improvement in the way young people and children in care are provided with the skills for independent living and advice and support with housing when they become adults and leave care' (Savage 2009, p.4).

Care leavers most vulnerable to poor housing outcomes

The patterns from follow-up studies and related research highlight key issues in respect of the group of care leavers who are most vulnerable to living in unsuitable accommodation. First, they are likely to leave their care placements early, often at 16 or 17 years of age, following a placement breakdown. Some of these young people see themselves as 'out of place' and 'pushed out' of children's homes and 'too old' for foster care (Dixon and Stein 2005, p.72). Leaving care early may also be a result of young people's expectations, wanting to be independent, 'I was 16, I felt ready and wanted to move on' (Dixon and Stein 2005, p.72). A survey of all 35 Scottish local authorities and the views of young people and workers also showed that young people may feel pressure to leave care at just 16, before they feel they are prepared or ready to leave (Scotland's Commissioner for Children and Young People 2008). The views of these young people raise issues about the role, culture and organisation of both children's homes and foster care in relation to preparing, engaging and supporting young people during their journey to adulthood, as distinct from their role in looking after younger children.

There is also evidence that foster placement breakdown may be a consequence of young people being unable to settle and commit themselves to their foster carers because of their unresolved feelings towards their birth families (Sinclair *et al.* 2005). Leaving care early is also strongly associated with young people being at greater risk of unemployment after care, which is likely to contribute to young people being in unsuitable accommodation (Wade and Dixon 2006).

Second, this group of highly vulnerable young people is likely to move more frequently for negative reasons. This may include an inability to manage in their accommodation, getting into debt, or not getting on with the people with whom they are living. Also, those young people who moved most frequently, for negative reasons, often found themselves in the most unstable and insecure types of accommodation. This included bed and breakfast, hostels, friends and returning to very difficult family relationships (Dixon and Stein 2005).

Third, frequent movement and instability, and poor housing outcomes are significantly higher for young people with mental health problems, emotional and behavioural difficulties, substance abusers and those involved in running away from care (Slesnick and Meade 2001; Social Exclusion Unit 2002; Vasillou and Ryrie 2006; Wade and Dixon 2006). Evidence from the United States suggests that the roots of these problems, often resulting in homelessness, may be related to the lasting effects of abuse, removal from the family home and lack of family support, rather than failures of specific preparation programmes (Park *et al.* 2004).

Fourth, young offenders leaving secure accommodation are vulnerable to poor housing outcomes and may be poorly prepared for independent living (Glover and Clewett 2011; Harder, Knorth and Kalverboer 2011; Youth Justice Board 2007). The main findings from a Barnardo's study by Glover and Clewett (2011) into young people released from custody included:

- The entitlements and consequent support for young people voluntarily accommodated (looked after under Section 20 of the Children Act 1989) drop off when they enter custody and resulted in unsupported and rushed transitions into the community.

- Young people who were 'looked after' and who were entitled to support saw themselves as forgotten about while in custody – and received limited help to plan suitable accommodation.

- A significant number of 16 and 17 year olds lacked sufficient support on release, which contributed to a disengagement from services and reoffending.

- A limited range of accommodation options for 16 and 17 year olds resulted in young people living in unsuitable accommodation such as bed-and-breakfast and hostel accommodation.

- Younger children, as young as 13, were being placed back with families unable to cope and with little support, resulting in homelessness some months after release from custody.

In response to this situation Barnardo's are recommending greater priority is given to suitable accommodation for young people leaving custody at governmental level, including 'a more comprehensive statutory package of support for *all* young people serving a custodial sentence' (Glover and Clewett 2011, p.50). They are also recommending:

- that former voluntary accommodated young people should continue to be 'looked after' on entering custody

- minimum standards and a quality assurance framework for temporary and emergency accommodation for young people leaving custody

- better inspection of resettlement support and pooled budgets to commission a range of supported and semi-supported housing budgets

- family support services

- national monitoring of the supply and demand of accommodation provisions.

The Barnardo's findings are complemented by two thematic reports prepared by HM Inspectorate of Prisons. The first report examined the contribution of young offender institutions to the resettlement of young people (HM Inspectorate of Prisons 2011a). It highlighted weaknesses in strategic management, case management, and in meeting the accommodation, educational, training and employment resettlement needs of young people. As regards accommodation, for those young people who could not return to their family, there was uncertainty for many young people about where they would be living very close to the time of being released – and a possibility they would have to register as homeless on release. For those young people returning to their family, there was a lack of work to maintain or improve relationships:

> In our view, some young people would be living in unsuitable arrangements with family on release but this was not addressed because of difficulties in arranging the alternative... In some instances young men were returning to an area known to be associated with their offending or gang links; it was not clear how this would be managed so they would not re-offend. (p.15)

The report also found 'there was no evidence that establishments were working to a set definition of suitable accommodation, although it is defined by the YJB [Youth Justice Board], or that discussions about suitability were taking place prior to release' (p.17). This contributed to the finding that case supervisors considered that a fifth (20%) of accommodation arrangements on release were not suitable or sustainable. A month after release, about half of the 22 young men for whom information was available, were in unsuitable accommodation: six were back in custody, one was 'on the run', two were in bed-and-breakfast accommodation, and living in hostels (HM Inspectorate of Prisons 2011a).

The second report focused on the care of looked-after children in custody (HM Inspector of Prison 2011b). It showed that 27 per cent of young people in Young Offender Institutions (YOIs) reported that they had spent some time in care (27% of young men and 45% of young women) – that is about 400 young people in custody at any one time who have spent time in care. The report identified these young people as a vulnerable population who are more likely than those who have not been in care to report problems on arrival, and problems with drugs, alcohol and mental health issues.

As regards resettlement, they were more likely than those who had not spent time in care to be concerned about finding accommodation and getting a job. The report showed that there was a lack of clarity about who had the lead responsibility for the resettlement planning of looked-after children and that young people were concerned about the lateness of making accommodation arrangements. The report recommends the need for a strategy for the co-ordination of services for looked-after young people in custody, clear procedures and a designated social worker in each YOI with responsibility for implementing the agreed procedures. It proposes the latter should include:

> offering advice and guidance to relevant staff in the YOI, and establishing and maintaining working links with local authorities to ensure that the needs of looked-after children are met while they are in custody and in preparation for release. (p.140)

How effective are leaving care services?

The numbers of care leavers living in 'suitable accommodation' aged 19 after moving on from their care placement has steadily increased from 77 per cent in 2004 to 90 per cent in 2009 (Department for Children, Schools and Families 2009a). Research studies adopting outcome measures show that leaving care services can make a positive contribution to specific outcomes for care leavers. In relation to accommodation these studies gave the following findings.

First, leaving care services are effective in assisting most young people leaving care in accessing housing. This includes: setting up a young person's accommodation on leaving care and liaising with housing providers (housing officers and departments, housing associations and voluntary sector housing projects) and acting as advocates for care leavers. The success of this process is underpinned by good relationships between the care leaver and the leaving care team, and good communication between leaving care teams and housing providers. It is also assisted by corporate housing strategies, formal arrangements and agreed protocols between leaving care services and housing providers (Dixon and Stein 2005; Ofsted 2009; Simon 2008; Wade and Dixon 2006).

Second, studies of initial access to housing and follow-up studies, show that most young people receive the accommodation they want on leaving care and have good outcomes after leaving care (Cameron *et al.* 2007; Dixon and Stein 2005; Simon 2008; Wade and Dixon 2006). In these studies positive outcomes were associated with:

- having access to 'good' housing on leaving care: those who failed to secure good housing arrangements early on tended to fare worse over the follow-up period

- having good-quality support in accommodation after leaving care

- receiving adequate planning and preparation prior to leaving care, so they had developed strong life and social skills

- being engaged in education, employment or training

- having a positive sense of their own well-being

- having a network of informal support, including family and friends.

Third, there is evidence that being settled and happy in accommodation after leaving care is associated with an enhanced sense of well-being, which is to some extent independent of young people's past care experiences or being unsettled at the point of leaving care (Wade and Dixon 2006). This suggests that housing has a very important and positive mediating role for young people leaving care.

Fourth, there is evidence, particularly in rural areas, of a shortage of housing and increased dependency on the private sector for provision (Ofsted 2009). Bed-and-breakfast accommodation is being used as a short-term measure to accommodate asylum-seeking young people and those whose behaviour is described as 'chaotic' (Ofsted 2009).

Fifth, the Care Matters stocktake showed evidence of wide variations between local authorities in the provision of 'suitable accommodation':

17 local authorities had all their care leavers in suitable accommodation, but 18 local authorities only had between 60 and 79 per cent (Department for Children, Schools and Families 2009).

Sixth, young people with emotional and behavioural difficulties, mental health problems, persistent offending or substance misuse problems and young disabled people are likely to have the poorest housing outcomes.

As detailed above, there is evidence that leaving care services and independent living programmes can assist young people when they get into difficulties (Collins 2001; Dixon and Stein 2005; Courtney and Dworsky 2006; Georgiades 2005; Wade and Dixon 2006). Even for those young people experiencing the greatest instability, continuity of support by services can prevent a descent into homelessness or allow a rapid escape from it. This is achieved in two ways: first, by the role of leaving care services in accessing a range of accommodation options, including emergency accommodation; and, second, by the commitment and ongoing support from leaving care workers in helping young people in sustaining their tenancies and being available to assist them at times of crisis (Simon 2008).

Summary points

- Children's services have a duty to accommodate homeless 16- and 17-year-olds under Section 20 of the Children Act 1989 and provide them with the full range of services under the Children (Leaving Care) Act 2000.

- About one-third of care leavers move in and out of homelessness over a two-year period. The provision of more emergency accommodation and better planning may prevent this happening.

- A smaller group of young people are more vulnerable to entrenched problems. This includes young people who leave care early, who move frequently for negative reasons, who have mental health problems and emotional and behavioural difficulties, and who leave secure accommodation.

- Leaving care services are effective in assisting most young people in accessing housing and in providing ongoing support, although there is evidence of variations between local authorities in the provision of 'suitable accommodation'.

- There is a need for early identification and prevention of problems, and agreed multi-agency interventions, including joint working between leaving care services, housing providers and adult services.

- Where problems persist during and after care, the evidence shows that there is a shortage of more specialist accommodation for young people with higher support needs.

Chapter 7

School Education – Laying the Foundations for Future Careers

I feel if I'd stuck in at school, if I'd got the right education at the right time, I could have gone further... I'm angry at other folk for not pushing me in my education.

Being in further or higher education or training, or settling in employment, represent important landmarks for most young people during their journey to adulthood. Preparing for a career through pursuing an educational or vocational course, or through an apprenticeship can lay the foundations of satisfying employment – and pay the bills as well! However, young people leaving care, as a group, may face a number of barriers in achieving their career ambitions which may begin within their birth families and communities, continue during their time in care and at school, and which may leave them ill-prepared at the time of leaving care.

This chapter focuses upon young people's experiences of school education. The significance of education in respect of improving the lives of care leavers in the longer term has been highlighted by the analysis of Swedish national registers for ten entire birth cohorts (Berlin *et al.* 2011). This research, the largest international study on this topic, identifies poor school performance as the major risk factor associated with future psychosocial problems, including poor career outcomes. The researchers conclude 'If society wants to improve the life opportunities for care leavers, it is necessary to give them effective help with their schooling and education while they are in care' (p.2496). This chapter will explore: first, what we know about the educational attainment of children and young people from care and how this compares with young people in the general population; second, the reasons for educational under-achievement at school; third, the range of initiatives introduced by government since 1987 to improve educational outcomes and their impact; and, finally, the contribution of the quality of care to improving the progress made by young people, so that they can achieve their potential.

School attainment

Research evidence dating back to 1987 and the collection of national data from 1999 in England has shown that many children and young people who are looked after have lower levels of educational achievement than children in the general population (Jackson 1987).

In terms of attainment, in England in 2010, at 10–11 years of age, 45 per cent of children looked after continuously for at least 12 months achieved at least Level Four in Key Stage 2 English and 44 per cent in mathematics, increasing from 42 per cent and 38 per cent, respectively, in 2005. However, these statistics compare with 81 per cent and 80 per cent respectively for the general school population in 2010 (Department for Education 2010c). Similarly, in 2010, 12 per cent of children looked after continuously for at least 12 months obtained five A* to C grades in GCSEs (or equivalent), including English and mathematics – an increase from 10 per cent in 2009. This figure compared with 53 per cent of all children (Department for Education 2010c).

Although there is evidence of some progress since data have been collected there is a significant attainment gap between looked-after children and all young people. In this context, in 2011, the coalition government introduced an 'impact indicator' to identify the attainment gaps between looked-after children and the rest of the population (Department for Education 2011b). This showed that in 2011:

- Forty three per cent of looked-after children achieved the expected level in both English and mathematics in Key Stage 2 tests. The attainment gap indicator between looked-after children and 'the rest' is 31 percentage points, a narrowing of two percentage points compared with 2010.

- Thirteen point nine per cent of looked-after children achieved English and mathematics at GCSE or equivalent at grades A* to C ('The Basics' at Key Stage 4). The attainment gap indicator between looked-after children and 'the rest' is 44.7 percentage points, a widening of 3.9 percentage points compared with the attainment gap in 2010.

The application of the Impact Indicator also shows that between 2007 and 2011, the attainment gap at Key Stage 4 has increased by 7.5 percentage points, from 37.2 percentage points to 44.7 percentage points. However, during the same period, at Key Stage 2, there is also evidence of a reduction in the attainment gap of four percentage points (Department for Education 2011b).

There were 5750 children looked after continuously for 12 months on 31 March 2011 who completed National Curriculum Year 11 during the 2009–2010 school year. Of these, on 30 September 2010, 70.5 per cent were in full-time education; 4.6 per cent were in full-time training; 7.4 per cent were in either full or part-time employment; and 17.5 per cent were unemployed – an increase from 14 per cent in 2008 (Department for Education 2011b). Government statistics also show that around three-quarters (73%) of children who had been looked after continuously for a year or more have some form of special educational needs. Over 1 per cent had missed at least 25 days of school during the previous school year in England (Department for Education 2010c).

The reasons for under-achievement

The Social Exclusion Unit (SEU), in their 2003 report, *A Better Education for Children in Care* (2003), identified five key reasons why children in care under-achieve in education:

1. placement instability

2. too much time out of school

3. insufficient help with education

4. primary carers not being expected or equipped to provide sufficient support and encouragement for learning and development

5. many children having unmet, emotional, mental and physical health needs.

The SEU report highlighted the evidence that young people in care were nine times more likely to have a statement of special educational needs than their non-care peers. Research has also shown the very high level of mental health, or emotional and behavioural difficulties among looked-after children and young people leaving care (see Chapter 9). The complexity of these mental health issues, and their roots, often lying within children's earlier damaging intra-family relations, and the failure of the care system to compensate young people, highlights the challenge in improving educational attainment, especially when normative measures of educational attainment are used as the main indicator. Some young people may travel a long way just to re-engage with education. This suggests the need for an understanding of the life course of children and young people in care for three main reasons.

First, most children in care come from very poor, socially disadvantaged family backgrounds and in addition have often experienced poor parenting, maltreatment and family breakdown (Davies and Ward 2011). Both these factors can contribute to educational under-achievement. Second, some young people's experiences of care may include placement movement and instability, which may disrupt their education and may be compounded by a sense of stigma felt by young people and low carer expectations (Stein 2005). Third, schools may fail to assist children and young people in care to develop their potential (Jackson 2002; Jackson *et al.* 2011).

Policy response from 1997 to 2012

Improving the educational outcomes of children in care has been a central platform of government policy since 1997. Initiatives aimed at improving the educational outcomes of looked-after children in schools include:

- The introduction of the *Quality Protects* programme in 1998 with the main aim of improving outcomes for children in need and in particular those looked after by local authorities. It included defined national objectives and performance indicators: Objective 4 was 'to ensure that children looked after gain maximum life chances from educational opportunities, health care and social care'.

- The introduction of national statistical data from 1999.

- *Guidance on the Education of Children and Young People in Public Care* published in 2000.

- Section 52 of the Children Act 2004 places a duty on local authorities to promote the educational achievements of looked-after children.

- Giving priority in admissions to looked-after children in the allocation of school places.

- Recognition of the Early Years Foundation Stage that looked-after children as a group may have additional needs.

- Provisions in the *Care Matters* implementation plan included the introduction of the 'virtual school head' with responsibilities for tracking every child in care in a local authority and ensuring that appropriate provision is in place.

- An allocation of funding to support the provision of personal education allowances to provide additional support in meeting young people's needs.

- The Children and Young Persons Act 2008, implemented from April 2011, placed the role of designated teachers on a statutory footing and introduced new provisions to ensure the education of children in care is not disrupted as a result of care placement moves.

- Under the *Care Planning, Placements and Case Review (England) Regulations 2010* and the *Care Planning, Placements and Case Review Regulations 2010 Statutory Guidance* (implemented from April 2011) local authorities have a particular duty to promote the educational achievement of the children they look after, regardless of where they live. This means they must consider the educational implications of every decision taken about the child's care placement. As corporate parents they must offer all the support that a good parent would give in order to ensure that the children and young people they look after reach their potential.

In 2010 the government reissued statutory guidance to local authorities on promoting the educational achievement of looked-after children emphasising the responsibility of Directors of Children's Services and Lead Members in respect of access to educational opportunities, the contribution of designated teachers, personal education plans, meeting individual needs and assessment.

Measuring the impact of policy initiatives

Judged solely on the evidence of how children in care compare with children in the general population, it could be argued that such a wide range of initiatives have achieved very little. As detailed above there has been some progress in recent years, when considering only the data on looked-after children – although as the House of Commons Education Committee Report published in March 2011 noted: 'the attainment gap between children in care and their peers has not narrowed and in some respects has widened' (House of Commons 2011, p.21).

The coalition government have committed themselves 'to doing all it can to narrow the gap in the educational attainment of children in care compared to all children' (House of Commons, p.21). They have highlighted the strategic role of local authorities in championing the needs of vulnerable children including children in care in the Schools White Paper, *The Importance of Teaching*. They have also supported the role of the virtual school head and designated teachers in raising the aspirations of children in care, and extended the pupil premium to include all children in care who have been looked after for more than six months.

The coalition government's *Positive for Youth* policy statement includes a commitment to: 15 hours a week of free early education for two-year-olds; the allocation of the Pupil Premium for pupils who have been looked after for six months or more; amendments to the school admission code to give priority to children who leave care under an adoption order, special guardianship or residence order; and an investment in junior savings accounts (of £200 from 2012) for every child in care who has not had a Child Trust Fund (NCB 2012).

What works in improving outcomes?

A knowledge review of what works in improving educational outcomes for children in care based upon research literature, key data and validated practice examples concluded that improving educational outcomes: 'will be linked with overall improvements in the quality of care that is delivered, and especially to children's emotional health and well-being' and that this should 'include focusing attention on all stages of a child's educational career, from early years through to support for further and higher education' (Brodie, Goldman and Clapton 2011, p.2).

The review was unable to find evidence in the studies reviewed of clear connections between recent initiatives and improved educational outcomes – 'A better understanding of their experience at school and as learners, together with consideration of other emotional and care needs, was required' (p.33). But there was evidence of virtual school heads, personal education plans and designated teachers as having a positive effect on the educational experiences (as distinct from outcomes) of children in care, and of better communication between social care services and schools.

There was also evidence of children and young people seeing their entry to care as beneficial in relation to their education. They gained from adults taking account of their learning needs, recognising when they needed help with specific subjects and, importantly, when personal problems were affecting their learning. This usually involves placements of a high quality, where carers have access to support from key professionals. For young people with very complex needs this may involve specialist therapeutic support and inter-agency collaboration (see 'Holding the Space' below).

HOLDING THE SPACE

BACKGROUND

This is an intensive therapeutic intervention aimed at young people living in residential care. Existing therapeutic services were finding it difficult to meet the serious emotional needs of this group and it was felt that a change in the culture of residential care was required.

Following a pilot, a two-year training course in advanced therapeutic skills for residential workers was developed. This ran over seven days in each term with additional training for whole staff teams. 'Holding the Space' has four components: a therapeutic group work method called 'the use of council'; Carl Rogers Core Conditions; the Creative Arts as Therapy; and Transpersonal Therapy.

BENEFITS

The training has resulted in visible change within the homes with improved relationships between staff and young people. Young people say they feel listened to and that they have better personal resources to deal with feelings of anger and sadness. External evaluation and inspection reports indicate that this approach to helping young people emotionally has had positive consequences for young people's education. Attendance levels are high and residential staff are good at encouraging and rewarding young people.

(Source: Brodie and Morris 2010)

Measuring the progress of children and young people

In the context of the wide-ranging factors which contribute to educational under-achievement of children in care, discussed above, using normative outcome measures (GCSE and Key Stage data) as the main measure of how well the care system performs is over-simplistic and very limited. These measures fail to recognise the very poor starting points on entry to care: not only do many of these children come into care in their teenage years from very deprived social backgrounds, but also many have experienced different forms of abuse or neglect, potentially casting a long shadow on their cognitive and emotional development. The education, careers, health and well-being of these young people will be far more shaped by what happens to them at home, in their schools and communities.

For those young people who remain in care longer term these official outcome measures fail to recognise the progress made by them, including major achievements, such as getting back into education, furthering leisure interests and vocational skills, and, often for the first time, developing consistent, positive and trusting relationships with adults. Research also shows that some of these young people do better by being in care, compared with stopping or returning home, which is not recognised (Wade *et al.* 2011).

This suggests that what is needed is a progress measure of what is happening to young people at different points in time that, in addition to performance, could incorporate their views of their well-being, as well as that of other important people in their lives. This would recognise the severe and hazardous journey many young people have taken, the efforts of those who have helped them, as well as more understanding of the complex roots and reasons for their vulnerability. It may also provide a more sophisticated way of identifying problems experienced by young people and a focus for intervention.

This was also the main conclusion reached by Berridge *et al.* (2008) in their study of young people with educational problems including those presenting 'behavioural, emotional and social difficulties'. The researchers argue that focusing exclusively on educational outcomes as a measure of progress for this group of 'difficult' young people is limited, as it fails to take into account a young person's family background, as well as the late age many young people enter care often with entrenched educational problems. The main implications for policy and practice arising from this study include the following:

- A wider measure of progress that takes into account a young person's behavioural, emotional and social difficulties should be adopted.

- Reducing movement and instability is helpful, as is a lower turnover of social workers; and more consideration should be given to the role and functioning of the children's home sector.

- Placement categories are not necessarily superior to others. What seems more important are the attributes of the particular individuals with whom the young person lives and the quality of experience that they offer.

- The delivery and impact of wider services are very important, including the school, social work, educational psychology and mental health provision. This included the positive contribution made by Educational Support Teams as outlined below.

THE ROLE OF EDUCATIONAL SUPPORT TEAMS

BACKGROUND

Each of the three authorities operated variants of Educational Support Teams (ESTs). These offered dedicated educational support for pupils who were looked-after children (LAC) – one comprised 25 staff, including advisory teachers and educational psychologists.

ESTs' services included monitoring the overall progress of pupils, such as establishing a system of predicted grades. One EST funded a national call centre, which each morning telephoned schools to see if LAC pupils had arrived. If not, it then contacted the placement to find out the explanation (e.g. illness) and, if necessary, alerted the EST to the absenteeism. They also organised achievement ceremonies to celebrate the attainments of LAC – these were very popular, often attended by local celebrities.

Another important role of ESTs was to offer training and support to teachers and carers. This included:

- running multi-agency training

- meeting with each new teacher and social worker as part of their induction

- organising education-focused summer schools and motivational schemes to encourage Year 12/13 (sixth form) study (including cash vouchers)

- offering a carers' resource centre, which loaned learning resources and provided advice

- supporting carers and Year 11 pupils in the weeks preceding GCSE exams – giving advice on completing coursework, revision strategies, exam skills and dealing with 'exam stress'.

There was also direct support for pupils including: newsletters each term; providing homework support; and helping to prepare home-study timetables and study packs for excluded pupils or those temporarily without a school place.

(Source: Adapted from Berridge *et al.* 2008)

The quality of care

There is research evidence that what can improve the lives of children in care, including their educational progress, is the quality of care they receive. The foundation stone of good-quality care is good social and psychological parenting. What is most relevant to the children and young people who are looked after in foster or residential care, is the research on the outcomes of parenting for children, and in particular, the work on parenting styles which underpins the parenting capacity domain of the *Assessment Framework*. It is the 'authoritative' parenting approach, combining love, emotional warmth, basic physical care, safety, stability, guidance and boundaries, stimulation, that is most likely to contribute to their all-round well-being. For looked-after children and young people, it is the foster carer or residential worker who gives meaning to 'corporate parenting'.

The essence of the 'corporate parenting' responsibility is to provide high-quality placements. This will require rigorous selection of carers who can meet the diverse needs of the different groups of children and young people who come into care, and who experience different pathways through care. It will also require policies, support services and training that will equip foster and residential carers with the skills to provide 'authoritative' parenting and at the same time not encumber them with unnecessary bureaucratic processes that may undermine their caring role and stigmatise the children and young people they are looking after. Providing children in care with high-quality placements will greatly benefit their education and lay the foundation stones for their post-16 further and higher education, training and employment (Sinclair *et al.* 2007; Stein 2009b).

Summary points

- There is an attainment gap between looked-after children and those in the general population and, although there is evidence of some improvements in the attainment of looked-after children in recent years, the gap has not reduced.

- The reasons for under-achievement are complex and require an understanding of the life course of looked-after children and young people, including parenting, social disadvantage, quality of care and education.

- A wide range of initiatives aimed at improving the educational outcomes of looked-after children have been introduced since 1997 including virtual school heads, personal education plans and designated teachers. These are having a positive effect on young people's educational experiences, as distinct from demonstrated outcomes.

- In the context of the wide-ranging factors that contribute to educational under-achievement there is a strong case for having a measure of progress, as well as outcomes.

- The provision of high-quality placements is critical to young people achieving their educational potential at school.

Chapter 8

Further and Higher Education, Training and Employment

> Well, me main problem is trying to get a job…yes, it gets me down a lot, 'cos you know there's nowt to do and nowhere to go…you can't do a right lot without money.

> I think I am special because I tried and finished college.

This chapter explores the post-16 career pathways of young people from care. In common with young people in the general population, some young people may leave school and go directly into employment, other young people may begin an apprenticeship or vocational training, and other care leavers may enter further or higher education. As discussed in Chapter 7 the foundations of successful careers are often laid while young people are at school.

This chapter will, first, describe what we know about how young people leaving care fare on these career pathways; second, it will introduce the legal and policy context, and, finally, it will discuss what research findings show about how young people can be assisted in achieving their career potential on their further and higher education and employment pathways.

The outcomes of career pathways

Government statistics for England show that the numbers of care leavers aged 19 with whom local authorities were in touch who were in education, employment and training increased from just under half (49%) in 2002–2003 to a high of just under two-thirds (65%) in 2007–2008 and since then it has dropped to 61 per cent in

2010–2011 (Department for Education 2011a). The proportion of care leavers aged 19 who were not in education, training or employment (for reasons other than illness or disability) has increased from 26 per cent in 2005–2006 to 29 per cent in 2010–2011 (Department for Education 2011a). However, despite the overall increase in care leavers in education, employment and training, there is evidence of significant variations in local authority performance. In 2008–2009 the proportion in education, employment and training ranged from 26 per cent to 96 per cent across English local authorities. Also, as discussed in Chapter 7, in respect of school education, official data show that there is what is referred to as an 'attainment gap' between young people leaving care and the general population of young people at GCSEs, A levels, and in the proportion of those studying at higher education (Department for Education 2010c, 2010d, 2011a, 2011b).

Care leavers are more likely not to be in post-16 education, employment and training than young people in the general population. In 2011 6 per cent of care leavers aged 19 participated in higher education, a decline from 7 per cent in 2010, and this compared with around 40 per cent of young people aged 19 in the general population. This decline contrasts with the general trend of increased participation amongst excluded young people (on free school meals) which has increased from 13 per cent in 2006–2007 to 17 per cent in 2008–2009 (National Care Advisory Service 2011b). There is also evidence of regional variation – only 3 per cent of young people in the West Midlands are at university compared to 11 per cent in inner London.

However, in 2011, just under a third of young people aged 19 were in post-16 further education, and since 2006 there has been a 28 per cent increase in number of care leavers at 19 in education other than higher education (National Care Advisory Service 2011b).

The legal and policy framework

The coalition government's policy on further and higher education, training and employment includes:

• Raising the cap on student fees for higher education to a maximum of £9000 per annum in conjunction with the production of Access Agreements by higher education providers for approval by the Office for Fair Access (OFFA). Care leavers have been identified as a specific policy target group by both OFFA and the Higher Education Funding Council for England (HEFCE).

- New funding arrangements for 16–19 year olds in education and training with a reduction of 74 per cent in funding for 'entitlement and enrichment activities' (entitlement covers tutoring and guidance activities; enrichment refers to social and cultural activities which are additional to core course provision) and an increase in funding for other activities including apprenticeships.

- The replacement of the £560m per annum Educational Maintenance Allowance (EMA) with a targeted fund of £180m for low-income learners aged 16–19 years of age. £15m is for care leavers and those on income support and £165m for a 'Learner Support Fund' to be administered by schools and colleges.

- The government's *Positive for Youth* policy statement includes a commitment to a 16–19 bursary of £1200 per year to looked-after children and care leavers to support them to stay in education, in addition to the higher education bursary of £2000 for care leavers, as detailed below (NCB 2012).

- The strategic responsibility for further education will remain with the local authority but the funding will be provided by the Young People's Learning Agency.

- The introduction of the 'Youth Contract' from 2012, which will include support for 16 and 17 year olds NEET, incentive payments for small firms to take on apprenticeships, and work experience placements for unemployed 18–24 year olds on Jobseeker's Allowance.

Local authorities have legal responsibilities under Sections 23 and 24 of the Children Act 1989 for 'maintaining' young people and providing 'financial assistance'. The legal framework is also accompanied by the *Transitions Guidance* on education, training and employment including needs assessment and pathway planning (see Appendix 2).

The Children and Young Persons Act 2008 provisions, implemented from April 2011, in relation to education and training include the following:

- Local authorities must pay a Higher Education Bursary of £2000 to certain former relevant children.

• Care leavers under the age of 25 who wish to take up a programme of education or training will have an entitlement to resume support from a personal adviser (PA) appointed by the local authority previously responsible for providing their leaving care support.

Improving post-16 educational outcomes

What does research tell us about how post-16 educational outcomes can be improved? Building on Jackson *et al.*'s study on *Going to University from Care* (2005), research from five European Union countries (Denmark, England, Hungary, Spain and Sweden) – collaborating in the Young People from a Public Care Background Pathways to Education in Europe (YiPPEE) project – has added to our knowledge. This identified 'facilitating factors', or what has helped young people succeed in their education, as well as the obstacles they face (see Table 8.1). The main findings from interviews with leaving care managers in England carried out by the YiPPEE researchers included a strong commitment to improving the educational attainment of young people they were assisting and encouraging them to continue in post-16 education or training. The researchers commented 'with some exceptions, expectations and aspirations for the young people concerned were rather modest and they tended to be steered towards vocational qualifications rather than academic courses' (Jackson *et al.* 2011, p.38). However there was a clear assumption that young people should be supported in their studies.

Interviews carried out by the YiPPEE researchers with a sample of 25 young people from England found that most were living independently in social housing and working part-time to supplement the financial support they received from leaving care services. The majority experienced severe financial difficulties and some were in poor housing in isolated or run-down areas. The young people also experienced far less support after leaving school and little assistance in their further and higher educational institutions – although there was evidence of ongoing emotional and practical support from former carers.

Table 8.1: Managers' views on facilitating factors
and obstacles for young people from care continuing
in post-compulsory education in England

Facilitators	Obstacles
• Placement stability	• Multiple placements
• Early support for catch-up learning	• Disrupted schooling and failure to compensate for gaps
• Action-oriented Personal Education Plans (PEPs)	• Problems in birth families
• Priority given to education by social workers and carers	• No emphasis on education or interest in school experience
• Personal motivation and persistence	• Low self-esteem and lack of aspiration
• Individual tutoring to compensate for gaps in schooling	• Lack of basic skills especially literacy
• Support from family, carers and professionals	• Poor conditions for study
• Financial resources and practical help	• Leaving care/independent living
• Sympathetic schools	• No understanding of care problems
• Positive community and cultural influences	• Knowing no one with higher education experience
• Clear protocols agreed with colleges and higher education institutions	• Lack of information and guidance
• Staying in placement after 18	• Rejection by foster carers, having no one who cares
• Leaving care team promotes education over employment, includes education specialist	• Anxiety about lack of money – few part-time jobs

(Source: Jackson *et al.* 2011, pp.28–39)

The research showed that most of the young people had experienced very troubled backgrounds, including poor parenting, abuse and neglect. Their experiences of care were mixed – some had very supportive foster carers, but others had placement disruptions (13 young people had between 4 and 10 placements) and young people reported a lack of interest in education in residential care. However, despite their negative family and care experiences 'many of these young people were able to maintain a clear sense of themselves as competent learners with…a strong learning identity. They looked forward to the next phase of their educational lives' (Jackson *et al.* 2011, p.40). As most of the young people came from families with no experience of post-16 education, continuing in education was made easier if this was the norm for the school, or they had friends who were aiming for higher education.

There was also evidence in the YiPPEE study of young people being involved in a wide range of social and leisure activities, including volunteering, which extended their social networks beyond care. It also provided some of the young people with support from adult mentors.

As regards their pathway to higher education, only three of the young people were able to follow a normative route: GCSEs – AS level – A level – university. The more common pathway was often delayed and disrupted and included: vocational qualifications – educational or vocational courses at further educational colleges, spread over time – university. For young people over 21 years of age there was also the option of access courses providing a direct pathway. In the context of delayed entry to higher education the authors comment:

> It is therefore essential that local authorities do not set arbitrary age limits on the financial support they are willing to provide for young people who have been in care to pursue their educational goals, and without which they will have little hope of achieving qualifications leading to satisfying or any employment. (p.44)

Recommendations from YiPPEE English Summary National Report

The YiPPEE study highlights the many barriers faced by young people in going on to further and higher education, which, as discussed in Chapter 7, begin within their birth families and extend into school and care. The study shows that many have the potential and motivation to succeed if provided with the 'facilitating' factors.

The study also makes recommendations for national government including the importance of collecting comprehensive statistical data. They also recommend 'Education and care for looked-after children should continue to be the responsibility of one central government department and of a single local authority department with a director of children's services at chief officer level and a lead elected member and a Virtual School Head' (p.44). The main recommendations for local authorities and children's services are detailed below. In England, the *Transitions Guidance* provides detailed advice on supporting young people in higher education (see Appendix 2).

RECOMMENDATIONS FOR LOCAL AUTHORITIES AND CHILDREN'S SERVICES

- Irregular school attendance should be recognised as a possible indication of serious family problems and information on unexplained absence should be more closely linked to safeguarding policies.

- A detailed educational assessment should be made when a child begins to be looked after and intensive catch-up help given from the earliest opportunity.

- Looked-after children should be retained in mainstream education with whatever additional support is required. Behaviour problems should be seen as a response to adverse experiences rather than an intrinsic characteristic of the child.

- It should be assumed that children in long-term care will remain in placement and education at least until the age of 18 and care and pathway plans should be formulated in line with that expectation.

- Foster and residential carers should be clear that promoting educational achievement is a key aspect of their role. Those not able to provide educational support due to their own low level of education should receive additional help and guidance from qualified teachers.

- Teachers need to understand the care system and social workers need to be well informed about education; this should form part of their respective training and continuing professional development.

- Leisure and social activities should be actively promoted and greater efforts made to ensure continuity across placement moves. More should be done to assist young people to capitalise on the opportunities for leisure-based and volunteering projects to provide qualifications, income and work experience.

(Source: Jackson *et al.* 2011)

Further education

As detailed above, there has been a large increase (28%) of young people in post-16, non-higher education since 2006. Participating in further education can be a very important step for many young people for several reasons: in getting them re-engaged in education, often after missing out at school; in giving them the opportunity to catch up and address earlier educational deficits; in providing young people with a normalising experience through integration with other young people, and opportunities to make new friends; and in providing a pathway to a career, and, for some young people, a stepping stone to higher education. However, as NCAS comment:

> Young people in higher education are able to access a range of universal grants and loans (available to all young people), but the same range of support is not there for further education, and access to courses is becoming more difficult. For example, funding for adult education has been reduced and the rules on who is eligible for 'fee remission' tightened. Thus more care leavers may struggle financially to access education without additional support. It is therefore important that both national and local government policies support access to further as well as higher education for care leavers. (National Care Advisory Service 2011b, p.8)

An evaluation of the Aimhigher West Area Partnership (Leonard 2011) made a number of recommendations for improving post-16 education for care leavers. First, the need for local authorities, further education colleges, the Connexions service and other stakeholders to work together, to develop information sharing and partnership protocols. The contribution of partnership working was also recognised by Ofsted (2009), as detailed below (see 'Support for care leavers: further and higher education'). Second, the need to develop the awareness of staff working in further education colleges about the needs of care leavers – for example through training programmes.

SUPPORT FOR CARE LEAVERS: FURTHER AND HIGHER EDUCATION

The Aimhigher programme helped raise aspirations and encouraged care leavers to think about following further or higher education courses. Two authorities had negotiated protocols with colleges and universities to help care leavers continue their education. In one authority, care leavers had fast-track interviews at college; in another, two universities agreed a reduced point admissions protocol for care leavers.

One authority identified that some care leavers dropped out in the period between leaving school and starting further education. In response, the Connexions worker based in the leaving care team provided targeted support during the summer break to ensure their retention in education.

Connexion service workers in all the authorities visited worked closely with leaving care teams, giving care leavers good advice and information and making young people aware of learning and employment opportunities.

(Source: Ofsted 2009)

Third, the evaluation recognised the important contribution made by the Buttle Trust's UK Quality Mark for Care Leavers in Higher Education and recommended work towards its implementation in further education – recognising its important contribution. The four broad Quality Mark criteria are: to raise aspirations and achievements; to have appropriate admissions procedures; to provide entry and ongoing support; and to monitor the implementation of the commitment from the education provider to ensure the needs of care leavers are taken into consideration, and the appropriate support is readily accessible.

Improving employment opportunities and outcomes

The poor levels of educational attainment of many young people from care, and the underlying reasons for their under-achievement, discussed in Chapter 7 and in this chapter, can have a long-lasting effect on the employment prospects of young people. This is reflected in the high rates of unemployment as well as unstable employment patterns after young people leave care. Research studies which have followed up young people for up to 24 months after they have left care, have identified the areas associated with good career outcomes, as presented below.

GOOD CAREER OUTCOMES

The following factors make good career outcomes more likely:

- educational success and continuous patterns of schooling

- foster care backgrounds

- encouragement by carers to achieve well

- either informal support by families and social networks or, for those lacking this formal support, by leaving care services

- leaving care at 18 or over, staying on in foster care

- having placement stability whist in care

- fewer moves after leaving care

- good housing outcomes

- strong life and social skills

- freedom from offending and substance abuse

- targeted career support.

(Source: Dixon and Stein 2005; Wade and Dixon 2006)

There is evidence that young people with mental health problems, emotional or behavioural difficulties are a highly vulnerable group – and are twice as likely as other young people leaving care to have poor career outcomes (Wade and Dixon 2006). The vulnerability of this group is explored further in Chapter 9. However, Tilbury *et al.*, drawing on social cognitive career theory, stress the importance of prioritising specific employment advice and support, as well as focusing upon care issues, such as instability:

> Many of the young people interviewed in this study were not in stable placements, but they still had future work-related goals and needed assistance to plan towards these goals. All of the domains of development are important, and while some needs may take precedence at a particular time, this is no justification for permanently creating a

hierarchy of need in which placement trumps everything else every time. Orientation to education and future work is an extremely important part of nurturing development of young people; it should not be relegated to second order for children in care. (Tilbury *et al.* 2011, p.351)

The authors identify four main implications of their study:

• Raising the aspirations of young people in care to achieve a fulfilling career.

• Improving their capacity to plan a career and to overcome barriers.

• Taking a longer-term and multi-dimensional approach to casework that is orientated to successful adult functioning.

• Responding more comprehensively to both social and psychological effects of the care experience (p.352).

In a similar vein, research from Canada also highlights the importance of a focused approach to raising educational aspirations, attainment and participation in education, training and employment (Flynn and Tessier 2011) Bilson *et al.* (2011) in their evaluation of employment schemes for care leavers in the north west of England identified the key elements of employment schemes as: preparation for employment and employability; work experience schemes; work placement and traineeships; apprenticeships; and mentoring. They stress the importance of further developing employment support by emphasising the employment needs of care leavers as part of the corporate parenting role; the need for collaboration between a range of organisations to develop employment packages 'co-ordinated by a single identified person who can offer continuity to young care leavers' (p.391); making an early start to employment and training planning – which may include a role for virtual school heads; the importance of collaboration at a regional level 'in providing support in the form of guidance as well as promoting trans-regional initiatives with employers and training providers' (p.392). The *Transitions Guidance* on employment and training is contained in Appendix 2.

In response to the high rates of unemployment of young people from care – care leavers are about three times more likely not to be engaged in education, training or employment than their peers – the government have funded NCAS to run the 'From Care2Work' project. This programme began in 2009 with the aims of improving the employment opportunities for care leavers, raising their aspirations and closing the gap between young people leaving care and their peers in the general population. Through working in partnership with local authorities and national and local employers it is succeeding in increasing employment opportunities. Between 2009 and 2011, 150 local authorities had signed up to the project and in total, 400 local and national companies were engaged offering 4609 employability opportunities, including 1096 work experience placements and 356 apprenticeships (National Care Advisory Service 2011d). Local authority provision has included: basic skills training (e.g. support for literacy, numeracy and ICT); pre-apprenticeship programmes (e.g. through work and college placements); pre-employment training (e.g. young people supported on business programmes); work experience (e.g. with council departments, help with application forms); apprenticeships (e.g. in business administration; customer services; health and social care); employment (e.g. young people being kept on as employees, after work placements); and post-16 further and higher education (e.g. academic mentoring, support with applications process, equipment, attendance at summer schools, visits to universities to raise aspirations). Between April and September 2011, 29 local authorities provided 3300 opportunities between them (National Care Advisory Service 2011d).

The project has also introduced the Care2Work Quality Mark standards, developed resources to assist practitioners and raised the awareness of the need to support young people in accessing and maintaining employment. Two examples of the project at a local level are presented, the Bradford Leap project and the Way Ahead project.

BRADFORD LEAP PROJECT

BACKGROUND

Bradford City Council's LEAP project (Learning, Employment, Advice and Preparation) provides a 12-week programme for care leavers and those making the transition from care who have found it difficult to engage with traditional mainstream services.

It aims to support young people who have found it difficult to engage with traditional mainstream services and prepare them for employment and increase their employability prospects. Young people attending the programme achieve accreditation in basic and social skills. Participants are supported by LEAP staff for up to 12 weeks (and beyond if required) after completion of the programme to track their progress.

PROGRAMME

The project also offers an intensive vocational preparation course to those less suited for pursuing an academic route into employment. An intensive four-day course is followed by a 12-week tracker period during which they are linked into work experience opportunities, traineeships or apprenticeships, within Bradford Council (as part of their corporate parenting commitment) or with external partners, and are given tasks to complete that demonstrate their development. Young people attend the LEAP programme for 16 hours per week and class sizes are kept small with employment (E2E) workers and a youth worker supporting each session.

Most recently the project has been successful in becoming an official satellite provider to Bradford College and is able to offer programmes that are both recognised and accredited by the college to those who are not ready for, or comfortable with, more formal learning environments. Within two years of its launch in August 2008, of the 49 care leavers who engaged in the programme 38 progressed onto further EET options and/or gained accreditation.

The staff who work within the project come from a social care background and all have a teaching qualification. Young people on the programme highlight their relationship with staff as 'key' and have said how they value the staff having an understanding of the care system and being around other young people from a similar background. The project has also shown how forging strong working relationships can lead to significant positive destinations for many care leavers.

(Source: practice example provided by
Bradford Leap project 2011)

THE WAY AHEAD PROJECT: SUPPORTING FROM CARE2WORK IN LEICESTER

OBJECTIVES

The project aims to develop a multi-agency, sustainable partnership to support and maintain care leavers in education, employment and training by:

- raising aspirations for care leavers

- developing opportunities for care leavers to improve their employability skills

- maximising EET opportunities for care leavers

- streamlining and co-ordinating pathways to EET

- celebrating success.

WORK STREAMS

There are a range of work streams linked to the project that come together to create an overall culture of achievement, aspiration and aiming high for our care leavers. These include:

- Way Ahead Project: a project jointly managed across Connexions and social care. The project manager has direct access to workers from both services, leads on career planning for LAC and care leavers, and co-ordinates a range of project activities and initiatives. The project manager is able to identify future funding streams which also support EET opportunities for care leavers.

- The project manager is the main contact point for the From Care2Work National Employability Initiative – Leicester has signed up to this national initiative and has been awarded a Quality Mark. The project has developed work placements in partnership with the Marriott Hotel (six placements four times per year). This model proved very successful and will be replicated with other private and voluntary sector organisations over the coming year thereby increasing the number of opportunities open to care leavers.

- Work experience placements are supported with the help of a voluntary organisation (Leicestershire Cares – Flying Fish project) who provide ongoing placement support and mentoring and work alongside the Way Ahead project.

- The project also supports work experience opportunities within the council – care leavers are a priority group within a corporate commitment to improving and increasing work experience and employment opportunities for young people across the council.

- Apprenticeship opportunities are being developed across the council, with care leavers having the opportunity to work in the 'family firm', by being supported to apply for these posts and given the skills to succeed.

(Source: practice example provided by
Leicester Way Ahead project 2011)

NCAS has also identified the general messages arising from the first three years of running the Care2Workproject (National Care Advisory Service 2011).

Corporate parenting in action

- Identify a strategic champion to get the employability of care leavers on the executive agenda, and bring together operational managers to turn commitment into action – all captured in a multi-directorate, multi-agency action plan.

- Consider how corporate parenting can be included in employment and skills strategies across the local authority.

- Create ways for young people to be involved in shaping services and monitoring outcomes.

- Ensure consideration is given to including meeting the needs of care leavers within any future funding bids to tackle worklessness locally.

A partnership approach

- Develop a network of internal and external partners, working together to create opportunities for care leavers to build their employability.

- Adopt the From Care2Work Quality Mark standards when developing opportunities.

- Ensure social clauses in procurement contracts are linked to corporate parenting responsibility to create opportunities for care leavers.

Raising aspirations

- Building employability starts with raising young people's career aspirations. We must develop a common language that puts building employability at the heart of planning and service delivery.

- Voluntary sector partners allow access to funding for activities that raise aspirations and help young people to discover their talents, for example Arts Council, Awards for All Community Foundation and other grant-making trusts.

Supporting the journey to work

- A dedicated specialist within the leaving care team provides a focus for employability, supporting young people to achieve their potential, and advising leaving care staff on education, training and employment.

- Building employability requires a range of opportunities to enable young people to access support, wherever they are on their journey to work – from achieving sufficient stability to engage with opportunities, to ensuring students in higher education are increasing their employability.

- All staff involved with a transition to adulthood have a role to play in supporting the journey to work, and may require training in order to increase current knowledge of career planning and building employability.

Summary points

- Care leavers have poorer post-16 education and employment outcomes than young people in the general population.

- International research has identified the main facilitating factors and obstacles to improving post-16 educational outcomes. The former include stability, staying put in placements after 18 years of age, action-orientated personal education plans, financial and practical help and support from family, friends and carers.

- The obstacles include: multiple placements, disrupted schooling and failure to compensate for gaps, problems in birth families, no emphasis on education or interest in school experience, low self-esteem and lack of aspiration, lack of basic skills especially literacy, poor conditions for study and knowing no one with HE experience.

- Research has also identified what can contribute to good career outcomes including building on educational success, encouragement by carers, stability, fewer moves after leaving care, being settled in accommodation and targeted career support.

- The From Care2Work project has provided examples of how to increase employment opportunities for care leavers through partnership working.

Chapter 9

Health and Well-being

I didn't know what was going on in my head because I was moving around so much.

Being in good health and having a positive sense of well-being is very important to young people in meeting the many difficult challenges of moving on from care to adulthood. It is very hard for young people to deal with the practical and psychological demands of moving into their accommodation, settling into work, or coping with the requirements of a new educational course or training programme, when they are anxious, depressed or ill.

This chapter focuses upon the physical and mental health of young people whilst living in care and at the time of their transition from care. This will include, first, a summary of the legal and policy context; second, an exploration of the health and well-being of children and young people living in care – as how young people are assisted with their problems whilst in care may greatly influence what happens later on in their lives; third, a discussion of what we know about the health and well-being of young people after they leave care; and, finally, a review of the implications for policy and practice, arising from the research findings.

The legal and policy context

Since 2007 there have been a number of policy developments, including guidance and regulations aimed at improving the health and well-being of looked-after children and young people leaving care. These include:

- A national indicator introduced in 2008 requiring all local authorities to provide information on the emotional and behavioural health of all children aged 4 to 16 who have been looked after continuously for at least 12 months. This data has been collected since 2009 using the

Strengths and Difficulties Questionnaire (SDQ) (see Dickson *et al.* 2010).

- The final report of the Child and Adolescent Mental Health Services (CAMHS) Review, *Children and Young People in Mind*, and the government's response to this report was published in 2008 (CAMHS 2008).

- *Statutory Guidance on Promoting the Health and Well-being of Looked-After Children* was published in 2009 (Department for Children, Schools and Families and Department of Health 2009).

- *Promoting the Quality of Life of Looked-after Children and Young People: NICE Public Health Guidance 28* was published in 2010 (NICE and SCIE 2010).

- *The Children Act 1989 Guidance and Regulations, Volume 2: Care Planning, Placement and Case Review* was published in 2010 (Department for Education 2010b).

- *The Children Act 1989 Guidance and Regulations, Volume 3: Planning Transition to Adulthood for Care Leavers* – the *Transitions Guidance* – was published in 2010 (Department for Education 2010a).

The previous Labour government also funded the Healthy Care Programme which supported up to 90 local authorities in improving the health and well-being of looked-after children through the development of local multi-agency partnerships. However, the coalition government withdrew this funding in 2011, causing the House of Commons Education Committee to comment:

> The government's support for a holistic view of the well-being of children in care is very welcome, but it sits oddly with the withdrawal of national funding for the Healthy Care Programme, which appears to embody this principle. (House of Commons 2011, *Fifth Special Report of Session 2010–11*, p.22)

The main implications of these developments for policy and practice are explored in the final section of this chapter.

The health and well-being of children and young people living in care

The foundations of good health and positive sense of well-being for young people after they leave care are laid earlier in young people's lives and are associated with how well young people are assisted when they come into care and compensated for earlier problems and difficulties.

Physical health

In 2001 the Office of National Statistics (ONS) surveyed the general health of looked-after young people (Meltzer et al. 2003). It found that two-thirds of all looked-after children and young people were reported to have at least one physical complaint including: eye and/or sight problems (16%), speech or language problems (14%), bed-wetting (13%), difficulty with co-ordination (10%) and asthma (10%). The ONS survey also showed that apart from asthma and eczema, physical complaints were more common among looked-after children than among children in the general population. Importantly, the ONS survey showed the close link between physical and mental health problems – over three-quarters of children with a mental health disorder also had at least one physical complaint, compared with just over a half of the children who were assessed as not having a mental disorder (Meltzer et al. 2003).

There is also evidence from the ONS survey that children living with their foster families are rated as having 'very good health' (69%), compared with children living in residential care (41%). The general health of children and young people improves as their placement becomes more secure, highlighting the importance of placement stability (Meltzer et al. 2003). Immunisation rates have improved for looked-after children. Government indicators for 2011 report that 79 per cent of looked-after children had up-to-date immunisations, rising from 76.5 per cent in 2005 (Department for Education 2011b). However, a lower percentage of children looked after continuously for 12 months aged 16 and over were up to date with dental checks and immunisations compared with younger children (Department for Education 2011b).

A UK study of children looked after for at least a year found that half had a physical or health condition of sufficient seriousness to require out-patient treatment, and over a quarter had more than one condition (Skuse et al. 2001). Also, analysis of data from the *Looking*

After Children: Assessment and Action Records reveals high levels of general unmet health needs; over half of the sample were identified as having health or behavioural needs (Ward and Skuse 2001). The Who Cares? Trust survey of 2000 young people looked after in England found that 40 per cent under the age of 11 felt that they had not received enough information about their development (Shaw 1998).

Two Scottish studies, one of young people living in a variety of residential settings and the other of young people living in foster care placements, found that the young people living in foster care reported themselves as being happier, healthier, eating better, exercising more and being far less likely to use drugs than their counterparts in residential care (Ridley and McCluskey 2003; Scottish Health Feedback 2001, 2003).

The mental health of children and young people whilst living in care

Children and young people often come into care with mental health problems. Data from the Looking After Children longitudinal study of 242 children showed that about 20 per cent of children starting to be looked after under the age of five years, had emotional and behavioural problems (Sempik *et al.* 2008). Analysis of the ONS data also found that by the time young people enter care many have experienced high levels of psychosocial adversity (Ford *et al.* 2007).

The ONS have carried out four nationally representative surveys of the mental health of young people in Britain (three surveys of looked-after children in England, Scotland and Wales) and one survey of children in private households (Meltzer *et al.* 2000, 2003, 2004). The first survey, carried out in 1999, obtained information about the mental health of 10,500 young people living in private households. The second survey focused on the prevalence of mental health problems among young people aged 5–17 who were looked after on 31 March 2001 in England. A total sample of 2500 within the age group was drawn, approximately 1 in 18 of all looked-after children and young people. The two surveys allowed for comparisons to be made between the two samples.

The older age group, the 11–15 year olds – who were most likely to become care leavers – were four to five times more likely to have a mental disorder compared with the private household sample: 49 per cent compared with 11 per cent (there were no comparative data on

16–17 year olds as they were not included in the private household survey). The rates for each broad category of disorder were: emotional disorders: 12 per cent compared with 6 per cent; conduct disorders: 40 per cent compared with 6 per cent; hyperkinetic disorders: 7 per cent compared with 1 per cent. As regards gender, in the 11–15 age groups, the proportions of young people with any mental disorder were 55 per cent for boys and 43 per cent for girls; for the 16–17 year olds the rate for both groups was around 40 per cent. At 16–17, girls had a higher prevalence of emotional disorders and a lower rate of conduct disorders than boys.

In terms of placements, two-thirds of young people living in residential care were assessed as having a mental disorder, compared with half of those living independently, and about 40 per cent of those placed with foster carers or with their birth parents (on care orders). The distribution of all mental disorders was significantly different according to placement. Children (on care orders) living with their birth parents or in residential care were about twice as likely as those in foster care to have emotional disorders. Children living in residential care were far more likely than those in foster care or living with their birth families (on care orders) to have conduct disorders. The prevalence of mental disorders tended to decrease with the length of time in their current placement.

The survey also established a close association between mental disorders and physical complaints compared with those young people who had no mental disorder. Also children and young people with a mental disorder were nearly twice as likely as children with no disorder to have marked difficulties with reading (37% compared with 19%); mathematics (35% compared with 20%); and spelling (41% compared with 24%). Over a third (35%) of children with a mental disorder were three or more years behind their intellectual development, twice the rate as among children with no disorder. Among the children with a mental disorder 42 per cent had a statement of special educational needs (SEN), twice the proportion found among the sample with no mental disorder. There was an association with having a mental disorder and truancy. Finally, the survey also showed that young people with a mental disorder were much more likely to smoke, be regular drinkers and use drugs than children with no disorders.

In 2007, Ford *et al.* combined the data from the four British ONS surveys to carry out the largest epidemiological study of looked-after children to date, using a random sample and including young people (aged 5–17 years) living in the full range of placements (Ford *et al.* 2007). They found that the prevalence of psychosocial adversity and psychiatric disorder ranged from 45 per cent to 49 per cent. This was higher than the most socio-economically disadvantaged children living in private households. Their analysis also showed that fewer than one in ten looked-after children and young people demonstrated particularly good psychological adjustment, as distinct from having mental health problems.

As regards 'care-related variables', they also found high rates of emotional and conduct disorder among young people living in residential care, or living independently, and associations between: psychiatric disorders of looked-after children and entering the care system later; more reported changes of placement within the past year; and having lived for less time in their current placement (Ford *et al.* 2007).

Between October 2008 and February 2009, Ofsted carried out a survey of 27 children's homes, including one secure home and a residential special school, in order to evaluate the provision of mental health services for young people over the age of 16 (Ofsted 2010). Their key findings, including the implications for improving services are outlined below.

MENTAL HEALTH SERVICES FOR YOUNG PEOPLE OVER 16 IN RESIDENTIAL CARE

- Some young people were severely disadvantaged because of differences in mental health provision across the country. In contrast, there was evidence of successful outcomes for young people who received specialist input.

- Inadequate assessments on admission to a children's home often led to delays for the young people in receiving specialist mental health support. This led to poorer outcomes for them and made it harder to call on specialist support when needed.

- Young people in specialist children's homes received appropriate specialist therapeutic care from competent staff with a good understanding of their specific needs.

- Access to CAMHS was inconsistent. Provision varied from a good service to none. Young people in local authority homes with a service level agreement were the most likely to access CAMHS easily. Access was generally worse when young people were living in a private children's home and placed outside their local authority. Thirteen of the 27 children's homes visited reported delays in a service being provided. Of these 13, 10 were privately run.

- Staff were able to provide consistent and continuous support when communication and working relationships between carers and specialist providers were good.

- Despite a lack of specialist training and qualifications, staff in non-specialist children's homes had developed a wide range of skills, knowledge and expertise.

- Good working relationships between the different agencies promoted opportunities for consultation with young people and a commitment to develop and improve local services.

- There were no suitable forums for representatives from the mental health sector to meet providers and managers of children's homes to monitor and evaluate services.

- Some of the young people had a negative attitude to mental health. This meant that they could miss opportunities to use suitable services.

- The transfer from children's mental health services to services for adults was inconsistent and sometimes led to services for young people being discontinued.

(Source: Ofsted 2010)

Young people's health and well-being after leaving care

Physical health

In relation to leaving care, there is evidence of increased physical health problems in the year after leaving care. Scottish research showed that 12 per cent of the young people surveyed reported having a long-term physical health problem, while almost a fifth (18.7%) reported having other health problems, such as asthma, eczema, hearing impairments or problems associated with drug or alcohol misuse (Dixon and Stein 2005). Saunders and Broad also identify the health problems of young people leaving care; just under half of their sample of 48 young people had long-term health problems. The young people surveyed felt that their health was affected by housing, personal relationships, their care experience, as well as 'depression' and their general feeling about life (Saunders and Broad 1997).

Mental health and well-being

An early English study (Saunders and Broad 1997) of 48 care leavers found that 17 per cent had long-term mental illnesses or disorders, including depression, eating disorders and phobias, but this represented nearly all the females (87%) within the sample. Just over a third of the total sample had deliberately self-harmed since the age of 15 or 16, either by cutting, overdosing, burning or a combination of two or more of these. Nearly two-thirds of the young people had thought about taking their own lives and 40 per cent had tried to when aged between 15 and 18 years, at the time they were leaving care.

Dixon *et al.* (2006) explored the outcomes of 106 young people who had left the care of seven English local authorities. The study focused on the first 12–15 months of young people's transitions from care to independent living, including their accommodation, careers, health, well-being and risk behaviour. Young people were interviewed within three months (baseline) of leaving care and again 12–15 months later, and, in addition, parallel information was collected from their leaving care workers. Both the General Health Questionnaire (GHQ-12) and the Lancashire Quality of Life ProFile including Cantril's Ladder (CL) were used to measure mental health and well-being (see appendix C, Dixon *et al.* 2006).

The study found that 10 per cent of young people had mental health problems at baseline, including depression, self-harming, eating disorders, anxiety attacks and episodes of paranoia. Also at baseline a high proportion of young people (42%) had emotional and behavioural difficulties, either moderate (41%) or severe (11%). These problems included anger management, verbal, physical or sexual aggression, hyperkinetic disorders, alcoholism, offending, mood swings and emotional problems related to their care experiences. Altogether (including young people who fell into both categories) 44 per cent of the sample was found to have emotional, behavioural or mental health problems. The study also found evidence of health-related risk behaviour including substance abuse (18%).

The study also provided evidence of an increase in mental health problems between the baseline interviews and follow-up, at which time young people had been living out of care for 12–15 months. Young people self-reporting mental health problems doubled (12% to 24%) and this included stress and depression, and four young people (4%) had made suicide attempts. Analysis of the GHQ-12 change scores also showed an increase in symptoms for 41 per cent of the sample, indicating deterioration in mental well-being over the follow-up period. Why should this be so?

Dixon et al.'s analysis of outcome measures suggests that coping with the demands of transition from care itself, settling in accommodation and their careers, often at a very young age, can combine with earlier pre-care and in-care difficulties (as evidenced above), or new challenges during transition, which affects young people's overall health and well-being (Dixon 2008). There is also evidence that mental health problems may increase over time for care leavers. Research carried out in Scotland found there was a fourfold increase in young people reporting mental health problems up to 11 months after leaving care, and this is also evidenced in international research (Dixon and Stein 2005; Stein and Dumaret 2011). Finally, HM Government's *Consultation on Preventing Suicide* (2011a) has identified looked-after children and care leavers as a highly vulnerable group, noting they 'are between four and five times more likely to attempt suicide in adulthood' (p.27).

Policy and practice implications
The role of the personal adviser
The *Transitions Guidance* highlights the pivotal role of young people's personal advisers. They have responsibility for ensuring that young people's pathway plans take account of their assessed health needs and set out how these are to be met. The dimensions of need to be addressed in respect of needs assessment and pathway planning, relating to health and well-being, include: 'health and development', emotional and behavioural development', 'identity' and 'family and social relationships' (these are detailed in Appendix 1).

The 2009 *Statutory Guidance on Promoting the Health and Well-being of Looked-After Children* highlights the vulnerability of care leavers to poor health and the important contribution to be made by leaving care services and the young person's personal adviser:

> Young people leaving care should be able to continue to obtain health advice and services at what is often a very stressful time for them. Personal advisers should work closely with doctors and nurses involved in health assessments and would benefit from training in how to promote both physical and mental health. (Department for Children, Schools and Families and Department of Health 2009, p.31)

> Leaving care services should ensure that health and access to positive activities are included as part of young people's pathway planning, and could consider using their premises to offer health services. CAMHS transitions should be planned at least six months in advance of the 18th birthday, in line with recommendations in the CAMHS Review. (p.32)

> Care leavers with complex needs, including those with disabilities, may transfer direct to adult services and the pathway plan will need to ensure that this transition is seamless and supported. For care leavers whose needs do not meet the criteria for support by adult services, their personal adviser should ensure that all possible forms of support, including that offered by the voluntary sector, should be identified and facilitated as appropriate. (p.32)

As detailed above, research findings show that young people's physical and mental health problems increase at the time of transition, arising from earlier pre-care and in-care difficulties, or new challenges during transition – health and well-being are closely connected to other dimensions of young people's lives including education, careers, accommodation, life skills and social support. As well as more gradual transitions from care, personal advisers will have a key role in either providing them with personal support or ensuring they receive the support they need which may including leaving care services, mentoring, support by former carers and positive family and kinship networks.

Health assessments and plans

A review prepared to inform the preparation of the 2009 statutory guidance (identified above) suggested the need for improvement in three main areas (Mooney *et al.* 2009): first, widening the range of topics covered in the health assessments – only just over one in five recorded information about family history, and there was a lack of information about the health needs of teenagers; second, using the assessment process as means to promote children's and young people's health – many assessments were seen as a disease-screening exercise, and third, ensuring the recommendations contained within the health assessments are carried out.

The review also identified the need to improve time-frames for health assessments and the variation in the quality of health plans, including a failure to consistently implement their recommendations.

Access to mental health services

As regards access to mental health services, the review carried out by Mooney *et al.* (2009) showed that young people often experienced delays and long waiting lists in accessing CAMHS, particularly when they were in out-of-area placements. They propose that the needs of looked-after children were best met by:

- a dedicated CAMHS for this group of young people, or dedicated CAMHS post integrated within a looked-after children team

- training and support for those working with looked-after children to meet their needs at an earlier stage, to help alleviate crisis intervention at a later point

- family support clinics run by nurses with mental health expertise as the first point of contact for carers and children with high SDQ scores from which direct referrals could be made to CAMHS

- services offered by Relate based in secondary schools

- at a strategic level, the review also identified the importance of good-quality data and needs analysis to inform the planning and development of services – or acting as a good corporate parent.

An example of good practice in this area is provided by the Peterborough Fostering and Adoption Clinical Psychology Service (see above). The service consists of one full-time clinical psychologist and one full-time assistant psychologist. It covers the areas of fostering, adoption, kinship, the needs of the residential units and where possible out-of-county placements.

THE PETERBOROUGH FOSTERING AND ADOPTION CLINICAL PSYCHOLOGY SERVICE

This team offers a number of services, including:

- Accepting referrals for direct assessment and therapeutic input with young people who are fostered, adopted, in kinship or residential placements.

- Consultation: offering psychological formulations and interventions regarding young people to carers/adopters and professionals (e.g. social workers, teachers).

- Training for carers/adopters and professionals.

- Joint work with colleagues within Peterborough City Council.

- Running groups for carers and adopters, focused on reducing placement breakdown, via psycho-education on mental health and relevant psychological processes.

- Recruitment, assessment and training of potential carers and adopters.

- Assisting in the matching of children to adoptive, kinship and fostering and residential placements.

- Facilitating referrals to local CAMHS and other health services, when appropriate.

By working in these areas, the team has been able to contribute to the identification of the mental health needs of young people in foster care, kinship placements, adoptive and residential placements, to make recommendations about how these health needs might be met and meet these needs directly via the treatment component of the service.

The main findings of the audit indicate that:

- Since the Peterborough Fostering and Adoption Clinical Psychology Service became fully operational (in September 2010), it has received 102 referrals and accepts between 12 and 18 referrals each month.

- A total of 113 carers/adopters and professionals have attended some form of training provided by the service since September 2010.

- The 12-month targets identified during the commissioning of the service were met and exceeded in six months.

- Seventy per cent of referrals were offered initial appointments within three weeks. This is well below Trust waiting list targets. Waiting times for treatment following assessment were no more than four weeks for any referral.

- The children receiving involvement from the service have less placement breakdown compared with national figures of placement breakdown.

- Feedback from professionals, carers and young people is very positive, with all three groups regarding the service very highly.

(Source: practice example provided by Peterborough Fostering and Adoption Clinical Psychology Service 2011)

There is also research evidence that Multidimensional Treatment Foster Care (MTFC-A) can reduce the behaviour problems of those young people with the most serious anti-social behaviour – although those young people who were not anti-social did significantly better if they received a usual care placement (Biehal *et al.* 2012). This is a highly structured intervention providing wraparound multi-professional support and including daily communication between carers, a specialist team and school.

Moving to adult services

Evidence from a review of research carried out between 2000 and 2011 identified the difficulties experienced by young people, including those from care, of moving on from child and adolescent mental health services to adult services (Brodie *et al.* 2011). The review identified the 'recurrent problems' which may lead to young people 'ceasing to use services until a crisis occurs' (p.1). The key messages for practice are identified below ('Mental health service transitions for young people').

These messages were broadly consistent with the analysis and recommendations of the CAMHS Review (2008). In respect of young adults who are approaching 18 years of age and being supported by CAMHS, the Review proposed: a planning meeting at least six months before their eighteenth birthday; having a lead person to ensure the transition between services goes smoothly; contingency planning, and 'confidence that services will focus on need, rather than age, and will be flexible' (p.12).

MENTAL HEALTH SERVICE TRANSITIONS FOR YOUNG PEOPLE

- Moving from child and adolescent mental health services to adult services is difficult for many young people, their parents and carers.

- Recurrent problems include limited participation of young people, high eligibility thresholds for entry into adult mental health services and inconsistent support during transition. This leads to some young people ceasing to use services until a crisis occurs.

- Service transition is a *process*, and needs to take account of the wider context of young people's lives, including education, employment, housing and overall health needs.

- Young people, their families and carers want their views to be taken seriously and to participate actively in the process of transition. They value good information, consistent support from a key worker and flexible, non-stigmatising community-based services appropriate for their age group.

- Good practice also involves collaborative flexible working between agencies, clear protocols and transparent planning meetings.

- There are limited adults' services for specific groups of young people, including those with attention-deficit hyperactivity disorder and autism spectrum disorders.

- Many practice developments and service models for improving transitions are at an early stage of development, and there are few robust effectiveness studies currently available. No research studies were found on costs or cost-effectiveness.

- Implications for service improvement include young people needing transitional support from CAMHS and voluntary sector agencies to help them adapt to the different culture of adults' services.

(Source: Brodie *et al.* 2011)

Summary points

• Many children and young people enter care with mental health problems. These should be addressed by comprehensive assessments, the provision of stable, high-quality placements and treatment interventions.

• Young people's physical and mental health problems may increase at the time of leaving care and this is associated with coping with the physical and psychological demands of accelerated and compressed transitions, combined with earlier pre-care and in-care problems.

• Young people can be assisted by more gradual transitions from care, ongoing support by their personal advisers, and access to mental health and psychological services.

• Young people may experience problems in moving from child and adolescent mental health services to adult services. These should be addressed by planning ahead, involving young people and carers, having a clearly identified lead professional, providing clear advice and information, and effective and flexible multi-agency work.

Chapter 10

Young People Needing More Support

> You need extra support and people to come and see you more...they should provide you with what you need, as your parents would...they take you away, they should look after you.

Most young people moving on from care, whatever their circumstances, will face many of the difficulties and challenges on their pathways to adulthood identified in the earlier chapters. This chapter focuses upon specific groups of young people whose needs or circumstances may result in them requiring *additional* support. This will include a discussion of the needs of disabled young people, young parents, young people from minority ethnic backgrounds, unaccompanied asylum-seeking children and young people, lesbian, gay, bisexual and trans-gendered young people, and young offenders and substance abusers.

Disabled young people

Living in care

Disabled children and young people come into care for the same reasons as other children – as a result of physical, sexual, emotional abuse or neglect (Sinclair *et al.* 2007). In England, at the point of being looked after at the end of March 2011, 2150 children (3%) had a need category of 'child's disability' (Department for Education 2011a). However, a review of different data sources in England estimated that disabled children and young people constituted between 10 and 25 per cent of the looked-after population – the use of different definitions and measurements mean that there is not an agreed figure (Baker 2007). There is evidence that disabled children and young people are over-represented in the care system as a consequence of their vulnerability to maltreatment (Gordon *et al.* 2000). As Baker suggests: 'They may be exposed to a series of different carers, have an impaired capacity to resist or avoid abuse…be less able to articulate a complaint, and workers may lack the necessary skills to facilitate communication' (Baker 2011, p.5).

Research comparing the experiences of disabled and non-disabled young people shows that on average disabled young people enter care at an older age, remain in care longer, are more likely to be male, are much more likely to display a high level of challenging behaviour and are more likely to be placed in residential care (Baker 2011). Baker has also suggested that disabled children may experience a reverse cycle of permanency, being less likely than other children in care to receive permanent placements including adoption and return home (Baker 2007).

Disabled young people also have a higher risk of being placed inappropriately, including in boarding schools 52 weeks a year, full-time respite care or adult residential facilities. There is also evidence of the increased use of 'out of area' placements by local authorities which means 'disabled children are likely to live further away from their families and communities, creating problems in monitoring placements and maintaining contact' (Baker 2011, p.7). As discussed earlier, good-quality care lays the foundation for young people's well-being and successful transitions to adulthood. The main implications arising from these findings for improving the quality of care for disabled young people are summarised below.

IMPROVING THE QUALITY OF CARE FOR DISABLED YOUNG PEOPLE

The findings suggest the importance of the following:

- Increasing the choice and quality of placements including return home, adoption, and foster care.

- Promoting stability in different care settings through high-quality assessment, planning and shared care.

- Providing ongoing reliable support to carers and young people.

- Carers needs for support services which provide relevant information, expert advice, and training, and are well co-ordinated.

- The opportunity for guaranteed breaks.

- Supporting positive contact between disabled children and their families.

- Listening to disabled young people as part of the assessment, planning and review process – having someone who can understand their views and needs if impairments affect their communication and understanding.

(Source: Adapted from Baker 2011)

Transitions from care to adulthood

There has been little research into the experiences of young disabled people leaving care even though, as discussed above, they are over-represented in the care system. Priestley *et al.* have suggested that there is almost no cross-fertilisation of knowledge between the literature on leaving care and disability (Priestley *et al.* 2003). Research into the experiences of young disabled care leavers moving on from care by Harris *et al.* (2002) and Rabiee *et al.* (2001) has identified the need for improvements in policy and practice. Their research has revealed a lack of planning, inadequate information and poor consultation with disabled young people and shown that young disabled people who did not have parents to argue on their behalf, or whose parents were not familiar with the system, were often disadvantaged in accessing the information needed to help them in making choices as they approached adulthood. Friends also often provided advocacy and support. Transitions from care for these young disabled people could be very abrupt or delayed by restricted housing and employment options, and inadequate support after they left care.

Rabiee *et al.*'s research found that the range of accommodation options was often determined by vacancies in existing adult services, rather than by the needs or wishes of young people. And for young people with 'mild' or 'moderate' learning difficulties there was a lack of support for independent living. Young people with 'multiple' impairments were more likely to move into residential care – as exemplified by Dawn, an 18-year-old young woman who was living in a residential home for older people (Rabiee *et al.* 2001). The same study also identified the gap between mainstream and specialist services that offered little middle ground for young people, particularly those with learning difficulties who were able to live independently if given adequate support.

As regards education, the study uncovered young people who had 'fallen out' of mainstream education. For other young people, in specialist provision, there was a failure to distinguish between education and social care, which impacted upon their employment prospects. Young people with committed parental advocates were more likely to obtain their preferred choice of school or college and less likely to be placed in non-educational day care alternatives (Rabiee *et al.* 2001).

With respect to independence skills the study stressed the need to link skills development with real life situations, avoid the low expectations often associated with impairment and care, and link skills with housing, transport, education and the use of money. The researchers comment:

> Independence should never be equated with doing things 'on your own'. Such measures will always devalue the independence of young people who use help to perform daily tasks. Making choices and exercising control over how things are done is a more significant measure of independence. (Rabiee *et al.* 2001, p.58)

The study also identified gaps in transitional planning resulting in abrupt transitions from care – including a loss in continuity in support and young people feeling lost, under-valued or pushed to make a move before they are ready. Other problems identified in the study included lack of consultation and involvement of young people, lack of collaboration between specialist and mainstream leaving care services, and other relevant agencies such as health, education and careers. Young people valued support from parents, relatives and former carers, which also had implications for transitional planning in the balance between formal and informal support (Priestley *et al.* 2003). Young disabled people were more likely to be dealt with by specialist disabled teams and may not be accessing mainstream services (Hai and Williams 2004). Disabled young people are also more likely to remain in their foster care placements after the age of 18 if they have the choice of supported lodging and adult fostering schemes (Sinclair *et al.* 2005).

It is also important to recognise any additional needs of disabled young people from black and minority ethnic communities as they make the transition to adult life (NCB 2011b). There is evidence that this can be achieved through multi-agency protocols, transition pathway information packs to ensure young people and their families from minority communities fully comprehend the transition pathway, and the participation of young people and their families in the planning process (NCB 2011b).

Disabled young people's transitions to adult services

Some disabled young people have more complex conditions and needs which require the involvement of adult services. Research has identified the problems faced by young disabled people in moving from children's to adult services. These include: poor co-ordination of services and lack of multi-agency working; lack of information for young people and parents; insufficient attention to the concerns of the young person; and a lack of appropriate services to which young people can transfer (Sloper *et al.* 2011).

Research carried out by Sloper *et al.* (2011) identifies the factors associated with developing and implementing multi-agency and co-ordinated transition services for young people (see below).

WHAT WORKS WELL IN DEVELOPING AND IMPLEMENTING MULTI-AGENCY AND CO-ORDINATED TRANSITION SERVICES FOR YOUNG PEOPLE?

- Having a transition worker who supported the young person and parents.

- The family having a written transition plan.

- The manager of the transition service having strategic level involvement.

- Transition workers setting up the adult care package for young people, negotiating the funding for it and supporting them until they were settled in adult services.

- Use of person-centred planning.

- Having designated transition workers.

- Having clarity on the role of the transition workers.

- Having parents on the service's steering group.

(Source: Sloper *et al.* 2011)

The transitions of disabled young people leaving out-of-authority residential school placements can be more problematic than the transitions of young people living with their families and attending local schools (Beresford and Cavet 2009). Recommendations for improving these transitions are identified below.

THE TRANSITIONS OF DISABLED YOUNG PEOPLE LEAVING OUT-OF-AUTHORITY RESIDENTIAL SCHOOL PLACEMENTS

Recommendations include:

- Earlier than usual active involvement in transition planning by adult social care staff.

- The existence of local authority posts with a specific responsibility for individuals placed out of authority.

- Local authorities considering making person-centred planning a requirement of placement contracts with schools.

- The development of systems through which adult social care agencies are made aware, at an early stage, of those in out-of-authority schools and their projected needs for adult social care.

- Early involvement of health services to plan transition pathways from children's to adult health services

- Better joint working between children's services and adult disability/health teams.

- The social needs of young disabled people playing a more prominent role in transition assessments and planning and in the package developed to support young people returning to their home authority.

(Source: Beresford and Cavet 2009)

A seamless transition to adult services will require overcoming major barriers arising from the existing legal, policy and organisational framework including: differing thresholds for eligibility for services contained within children's and adult's legislation; differences in the age criteria for transferring from children's to adult services (e.g. from child to adult health services at 16, from child to adult social care services at 18); and differences in organisational cultures between children and adult services, especially, where there may be a gap between a clinical and counselling orientation.

Both the 2009 *Statutory Guidance on Promoting the Health and Well-being of Looked-After Children* and the *Transitions Guidance* identify the need for disabled care leavers transitions to adult services to be seamless and supported. The young person's needs assessment and pathway plan is important to this process. The *Transitions Guidance* proposes a 'personal centred planning' approach: 'the young person must be kept at the centre with family members, carers and friends being partners in supporting the young person to achieve their potential' (p.35).

Although the Children and Young Persons Act 2008 makes provision for young people resuming education and training to continue to receive support from their personal advisers up to 25 years of age, those young people with the most complex needs, including mental health problems, who may not be in education or training, will only be supported by leaving care services until they are 21 years of age.

Overcoming these barriers will be necessary to assist young people's transitions from children's services to adult services. This will require a comprehensive response, including 'personal centred planning' at an individual level, and the introduction of 'joint protocols' at a strategic and operational level. As detailed in the *Transitions Guidance*:

> It is essential that specific protocols and agreements are drawn up in each local authority area, with the participation of all agencies. This will include children's and adult social care, children's and adult health, education, housing, youth offending, information, advice and guidance services, supported employment services and leisure services. (p.35)

Young parents

Although the numbers are small and there has been limited research, the evidence shows that young people in, or leaving, care are at heightened risk of teenage pregnancy. In England, there were 350 mothers aged 12 and over looked after in March 2011, a decrease from 390 in 2010; 46 per cent were aged 15 or under at the time of the birth of their first child and just over a third (35%) were 16 (Department for Education 2011a). An in-depth study of 101 young people leaving care in England reported 'a remarkably high' number of young parents: one in seven young people already had or were expecting a child whilst living in care and within nine months of leaving care, this had risen to over one quarter of young people, all by the age of 17 years – nearly four times the national comparative data cited in the study (Dixon *et al.* 2006).

These findings are also reflected in international research. A review of four Australian studies showed that just under a quarter of care leavers had children soon after leaving care, which was approximately 24 times higher than the rate of teenage pregnancy in the general population (cited in Mendes 2009). Research in the United States found that nearly half of 19-year-old care leavers had become parents at 19 years of age, more than twice the number of 19 year olds who had given birth in the general population (Courtney and Dworsky 2006). A Swedish study by Vinnerljung *et al.* (2007) based on 50,000 young people showed that 16–19 per cent of young women and 5–6 per cent of young men who had been in care became teenage parents. Care leavers were 2 to 5 times more likely than other young people to become parents before the age of 20.

Reasons for young parenthood

Barn and Mantovani (2007) explored the risk factors associated with young parenthood in a group of 55 young mothers from care. Their study showed high levels of family disruption, with long spells in care, lack of continuity of care and being placed in residential care. Family disruption was found to be associated with poor parental supervision and living in residential care provided opportunities for young people to be engaged in risky behaviour. In both residential and foster care the study showed that young women 'pushed the boundaries' but often weren't challenged, which translated into the young women 'feeling left to their own devices, with consequent lack of educational motivation or aspirations' (p.14). The study also found that many of the young women had poor school attendance and missed out on sex and relationships education. The impact of family rejection, and care, may mean 'distinguishing between a loving relationship and a sexual relationship may be difficult; therefore they may become exposed to more abuse and abuse through prostitution' (p.14).

A review of the literature carried out by Mendes (2009) suggests that the reasons for the higher rate of pregnancy and parenthood among care leavers are associated with young people's experiences before coming into care, including the psychological consequences of physical, sexual or emotional abuse or neglect; their experiences of care including instability and poor-quality placements; a lack of consistent and positive adult support; risk-taking behaviour; school exclusion or low achievement; and peer pressure in children's homes. As a consequence, Mendes suggests 'Many young people in care appear to feel unloved and unwanted and view sex as a means of attaining love and affection' (p.13). As regards policy and practice implications, he highlights the importance of:

• stability and continuity in care

• teenage pregnancy preventative programmes and access to birth control

• more gradual transitions from care and

• after-care programmes and support.

Consequences of young parenthood

Research findings on young parenthood in the general population have shown that young parents and their children are more likely to experience long-term social exclusion and poor outcomes compared with their peers.

Dixon et al. (2006) found that those young people in their study who went on to become parents were more likely to have had unsettled care careers including placement movement, running away, offending and substance abuse, and to have been unemployed. However, Barn and Mantovani (2007), Dixon et al. (2006) and Chase and Knight (2006) in their studies also highlight the positive experience of parenthood: it was mostly welcomed, brought pride and joy, gave a new sense of purpose and a feeling of being needed, sometimes compensating for their own experiences of poor parenting; for some young people it led to an improvement in their relationships with their families, including practical help and support, and increased support from foster carers.

Supporting young parents

The Foyer Federation has carried out a survey to identify good practice in enhanced housing support for teenage parents (Foyer Federation 2011). This included the provision of floating support, supported lodgings and supported accommodation. As regards floating support, good practice involved good relationships with other services, engaging and involving young people, including young fathers, and having well-trained and competent staff.

The strengths of supported lodgings were seen as being rooted in the communities of the teenagers they support and in being able to offer an informal approach. As a lodging host commented it is a 'non-intrusive positive role model and a listening ear that increases self-esteem and a belief that she can cope' (p.8). However, the survey indicated that it may not be appropriate for teenage parents with higher levels of need, including where there are child protection concerns (Foyer Federation 2011).

The teenage supported housing projects were seen as being able to improve outcomes for teenage parents but it was recognised that 'understanding conditionality in terms of incentives and opportunities rather than sanctions may prove useful when dealing with this particular group, whose extreme vulnerability (and the vulnerability of their children) makes imposing additional sanctions inappropriate' (p.19).

The main issues arising from the studies discussed above for assisting young parents are summarised below.

SUPPORTING YOUNG PARENTS

The main issues arising were:

- the involvement of leaving care services which is seen as very positive by young parents and particularly welcomed by young parents who are socially isolated

- young parents wanting to feel that the worker were interested in assisting them and not just interested in monitoring the care and protection of their child

- finances to purchase clothes and equipment

- pre-natal classes, birth information

- parenting skills

- involving young fathers in the birth and parenting process

- finding suitable accommodation

- accessing additional personal and professional support, for example, mutual support groups, mentoring and advocacy schemes by mothers who were formerly in care.

Young people from minority ethnic backgrounds

In England in 2011, 77 per cent of children in care were of white origin; 9 per cent were of mixed origin; 5 per cent were Asian or Asian British; 7 per cent were black or black British; and 2 per cent were from other ethnic groups (Department for Education 2011a). There appears to have been an increase in the numbers and proportion of looked-after children of Asian origin from 2100 (3%) in 2005, 2333 (4%) in 2007 to 3090 (5%) in 2011 (Department for Education 2010d, 2011a).

Differences between ethnic groups

Research has shown that black and minority ethnic (BME) young people, including those of mixed heritage, face similar challenges to white young people leaving care, and that there are few significant differences in terms of their care careers, in the manner or timing of leaving care, in their outcomes up to nine months after leaving care, or in the support available to them from professionals, family or friends (Dixon et al. 2006).

Barn et al.'s (2005) study of 361 care leavers, including 116 (45%) from a minority ethnic background, also highlighted the similar experiences of both groups on leaving care. But there were some differences. The researchers found that white, Caribbean and mixed-parentage young people were at high risk of disadvantage. For some Caribbean young people, placements in families which reflected their own ethnic background contributed to stability and countered the effects of disruption. School exclusion, placement instability and lack of encouragement and support contributed to the poor educational outcomes of white, Caribbean and mixed-parentage young people. But the help and support after leaving care was seen as variable and often lacking in focus and effect. The study also found evidence of asylum-seeking young people showing resilience and determination and doing well in education, and many of the Caribbean, African and Asian young people feeling secure in their individual and group identity (Barn et al. 2005).

Identity issues

Early research by Biehal et al. (1995) suggested that young people's definitions of their ethnic identity were often complex, varied and shifted over time. Their identification with a particular ethnic group was strongly related to young people's identification with or rejection of family members. Close family links, integration within the local black community, placements with black carers and reinforcement by parents or peers generally contributed to a positive sense of black identity. But some of the mixed-heritage young people felt that black or white people did not accept them – although they could feel secure about their identity (Biehal *et al.* 1995).

Dixon *et al.* (2006) found that young people did not feel distanced or isolated from their own communities and 'most had developed positive links, where they wanted them, and felt quite comfortable with their identities – a young black girl…there's no problem with that, I know who I am' (p.209). The study showed that most young people based their friendships on shared interests and understandings irrespective of race and culture.

Supporting young people

In Dixon *et al.*'s study, the local authorities did not provide specific services to meet any additional needs, but where staff teams were ethnically diverse this was welcomed by young people, having their needs met as part of an integrated generic service. There is some evidence that young people from black and minority ethnic communities are under-represented as CAMHS service users and that they are likely to reach crisis point before they come into contact with services (Malek 2011; Malek and Joughlin 2004). Malek has also highlighted the significant concerns BME young people have about racism, racist bullying and racial harassment, and the failure to recognise these as risk factors (Malek 2011). Additional support needs, identified from the research studies discussed above, are summarised below.

SUPPORTING BLACK AND MINORITY YOUNG PEOPLE

Research has shown that BME young people, including those of mixed heritage, face many similar challenges to white young people leaving care. However it is important to recognise and respond to:

- differences between different ethnic groups
- the complexity of identity issues and providing young people with opportunities to explore issues relevant to their own definitions – rather than imposing stereotypes

---

- the impact of racism upon young people

- the importance of family, friendship and community links – building on positive relationships as seen by young people

- the question of having ethnically diverse staff in leaving care teams

- mental health problems when they first arise and the importance of early interventions.

Unaccompanied asylum-seeking children and young people (UASC)

Official data

The large majority of 'unaccompanied asylum-seeking children' (UASC) – that is those arriving in the UK unaccompanied by a parent or responsible adult – are referred to local children's services departments for help. There were 2680 UASC who were looked after on 31 March 2011, a decrease of 22 per cent from 2010. The figures for 2003 and 2006 were 2200 and 3400, respectively. The proportion of looked-after UASC who were male was 89 per cent in 2011, the same as in 2010. The majority of looked-after UASC are aged 16 years or over; 75 per cent were in this age group in 2011, an increase from 70 per cent in 2010.

In 2011 the majority of looked-after UASC came from an Other Asian background; 43 per cent of all UASC are recorded as being in this category in 2011. Only 15 per cent of UASC were of black African origin, the same as in 2010. In 2007 most UASC came from a black African background with 31 per cent of looked-after UASC being recorded in this category (Department for Education 2011a). In 2010, UASC accounted for about 6 per cent of the care population in England but in London and the South East of England they represent a greater proportion of the care population: they constitute 17 per cent of looked-after young people in London (Department for Education 2010d).

Young people's experiences

There is limited research exploring the reasons for flight or the ordinary lives of young people before they become asylum seekers. The small number of studies that have been carried out show the main reasons for flight include: death or persecution of family members; persecution of the young person; forced recruitment; war; trafficking; and seeking education (Sirriyeh 2011). Most of the young people have a 'passive' role in the process – decisions being made by family, relatives, friends or neighbours and young people being accompanied by an agent during their journey. The journeys can be long and hazardous and young people can be exploited and abused by their agents (Sirriyeh 2011).

Research by Thomas et al. (2004) on the pre-flight experiences of 100 unaccompanied young people showed that most young people had experienced violence (86) or had witnessed the death of family members (13), suffered sexual violence (32) or lived in hiding (16). The impact of these 'trauma events' combined with post-settlement difficulties, contributes to an elevated risk of anxiety and depressive symptoms (Bean et al. 2007; Hodes et al. 2008; McKelvey and Webb 1995). As Wade (2011) has commented, 'this same body of literature also emphasises the resilience and capacity of many unaccompanied young people to meet the challenges of resettlement and it is with this combination of uncertainty, difficulty and capability that young people first seek help from children's services' (Kohli and Mather 2003; Wade, Mitchell and Baylis 2005).

Response of children's services

Earlier research, prior to 2003, showed that unaccompanied asylum-seeking young people were likely to receive poorer housing (including being put in bed-and-breakfast accommodation) and other services than looked-after young people, especially in respect of support from leaving care teams (Hai and Williams 2004; Stanley 2001).

Subsequent research has identified distinctive care pathways for unaccompanied young people according to age, with younger children tending to enter foster or residential care under Section 20 of the Children Act 1989 and a much larger group of older young people (mostly aged 15–17 at arrival) being supported in the community under Section 17 provisions. This latter group were found to be significantly disadvantaged with respect to quality of accommodation, educational progress and social work support, including access to leaving care services (Wade *et al.* 2005).

Department of Health (2003) guidance on the appropriate use of Section 17 accommodation and the findings of the Hillingdon Judicial Review have led to improved access to Section 20 accommodation and leaving care services. Some evidence of early progress was found in 2005 (Refugee Council 2005), and research into the fostering experiences of unaccompanied young people suggests there is now a predominant use of Section 20 accommodation and that most young people are able to access leaving care services, at least until their right to remain is removed. However, young people placed in independent settings continue to face greater adversity than those in more highly supported accommodation. This includes evidence of high levels of unmet mental health needs and their transitions being affected by their asylum claims (Chase *et al.* 2008; Wade 2011). Drawing on research studies, Sirriyeh (2011) identifies 'implications for practice' (see below).

UNACCOMPANIED ASYLUM-SEEKING CHILDREN: IMPLICATIONS FOR PRACTICE

SOCIAL WORKERS AND FOSTER CARERS

Social workers have an important role to play in preparing and supporting young people leaving care using multi-dimensional planning in the context of the uncertainty of young people's immigration status:

- Young people need support in accessing good-quality legal representation for their asylum applications.

- Education needs to be part of a wider comprehensive support package provided to young people. Where young people have strong networks of informal supports they tend to do better in education.

- Young people need support in accessing therapeutic support, although this is not necessarily needed by all young people. Consistent care and support can help promote young people's resilience and capacity to cope in the context of forced migration.

SENIOR MANAGERS

- Young people's feedback on foster care indicates that a broad view of matching is helpful, including the idea of matching according to cultural needs, but also balancing this with other aspects of young people's identities and needs.

- It is important to ensure that foster carers and supervising social workers are provided with training on some of the particular issues in working with unaccompanied minors.

(Source: Sirriyeh 2011)

Pearce (2011) has identified the problems facing practitioners in responding to the needs of trafficked young people. These include 'hidden' child protection needs; young people being passed between different agencies; immigration concerns taking precedence over young people's safety needs, equally meeting the needs of both internally and internationally trafficked young people, and, more generally, the importance of recognising the needs of older children within safeguarding (Pearce 2011).

Effective multi-agency working is essential in assisting trafficked young people as shown by the example above from Gatwick Children's Services.

TRAFFICKED YOUNG PEOPLE: IMPROVING LOCAL PROVISION THROUGH MULTI-AGENCY WORKING

- Our trafficked young people mainly enter the UK via Gatwick Airport. We work in partnership with immigration officers at the airport to identify children who may fit the profile of a trafficked young person, and with immigration police, who try to secure information about possible traffickers that could lead to a criminal prosecution.

- Gatwick Children's Services provides an experienced duty social worker daily, to cover the airport and provide advice, assistance and joint working on immigration interviews.

- Once the young person has completed their interviews with immigration, Children's Services transport the young person to a safe foster placement or supported lodgings provider.

- Within 24 hours we arrange and conduct strategy discussions with our local West Sussex Police Child Protection Team (PCPT) to look at the potential risks to the young person and how we can minimise those risks, whilst joint police, immigration and Children's Services enquiries and assessments continue.

- Following the strategy meeting with professionals we meet with the young person and an interpreter to explain who we are, how we are going to help and our concerns about the different types of exploitation they may be exposed to (e.g. domestic servitude, prostitution, slave labour, etc.).

- To keep them safe we ask for their written consent to share information with professionals, to take DNA samples and photographs, and ask for their consent to comply with a safety plan, which means no contact with people they may have telephone numbers for, no internet use and being accompanied by carers wherever they go, to school/shops, etc. for a period of a few weeks, until we are satisfied that risks to safety have been minimised.

- If young people do not sign up to the safety plan, as it is voluntary, we still do our best with carers to safeguard that young person's welfare.

- We also refer trafficked young people to the UKHTC (United Kingdom Human Trafficking Centre), as this can sometimes generate a positive outcome in their asylum claim.

- We work with and provide training to our supported lodging providers and foster carers in working with young people and how to manage the intensive safety plan requirements within the first few weeks of a young person's arrival. This has worked to very good effect and has seen a reduction in the number of trafficked young people who have gone missing from our care.

(Source: practice example provided by Gatwick Children's Services, West Sussex County Council)

In response to these issues, the government have issued Practice Guidance to assist those working with trafficked young people (HM Government 2011b).

The *Transitions Guidance* identifies the additional needs of UASC making the transition from care to adulthood by their having both a 'leaving care' and 'immigration' status:

> Pathway planning for the majority of UASC who do not have permanent immigration status should initially take a dual or triple planning perspective, which, over time, should be refined as the young person's immigration status is resolved. Planning may be based on:
>
> - A transitional plan during the period of uncertainty when the young person is in the United Kingdom without permanent immigration status.
>
> - Longer-term perspective plan in the United Kingdom should the young person be granted long-term permission to stay (for example through the grant of Refugee Status), or
>
> - A return to their country of origin at any appropriate point or at the end of the immigration consideration process, should that be necessary because the young person decides to leave the United Kingdom or is required to do so.
>
> (*Transitions Guidance* 6.22, p.39)

As detailed in the *Transitions Guidance* the role of the personal adviser and pathway planning is pivotal at every stage including:

- Work with the young person's legal representative and the dedicated case owner at the UK Border Agency to ensure that the young person understands the process of claiming asylum, the possible outcomes and to provide them with necessary support.

- Providing ongoing support in response to the outcome of the asylum claim – whether granted 'refugee status', 'human protection status', 'discretionary leave', or where the UASC are refused asylum with no grant of leave.

The personal adviser will have an important role in exploring the implications of the outcome for individual young people, where young people are able to remain for either three or five years, in terms of financial support, accommodation, funding arrangements for education, employment and training. They may also have to work with young people who are refused asylum in planning for a return to their country of origin, usually in collaboration with the UK Border Agency. Wade (2011) has highlighted the demands of this work for practitioners and in particular those arising from dealing with uncertainty:

> Assessments are complicated by uncertainty about young people's ordinary lives before leaving, the absence of external information and the understandable suspicion and confusion that young people bring with them to these encounters. While some stories may be satisfactorily revealed over time, others may not. Pathway planning is equally subject to uncertainty. On a large canvass, uncertainty derives from the continuously shifting nature of government immigration policy. For individual young people, uncertainty arises from the asylum determination process. (p.2429)

Lesbian, gay, bisexual and trans-gendered young people

There has been very little UK research on the support needs of lesbian, gay, bisexual and trans gendered young people (LGBT) from care. In England, only Broad, in his policy surveys carried out before and after the introduction of the Children (Leaving Care) Act 2000, identifies 'gay and lesbian initiatives', as part of 'anti-discriminatory practice and policies in leaving care work' (Broad 2005). Broad's findings show that generally, anti-discriminatory policies have much less impact on practice than team policies and case-by-case decisions. There is also evidence from Scotland that a third of local authorities reported having programmes for dealing with sexual health and/or sexuality (Dixon and Stein 2005).

Drawing on research from the United States, Smith (2011) identifies a number of important issues:

- LGBT young people may have been rejected by their birth families due to their sexual orientation or gender identity, or they may disclose their sexual orientation or gender identity while in care.

- If they are rejected by their birth families they may not return home or may lack permanent connections to their families and communities.

- They may run away from care and experience unstable placement histories due to staff discomfort with their sexual orientation.

- They may be more likely to be placed in residential care, be less likely to receive services and be more likely to be physically and sexually abused.

- One study of LGBT young people in New York City homes found that all of the young people reported verbal harassment by peers, staff and other providers, 70 per cent reported physical violence, and 56 per cent reported living on the streets for a while because they felt safer there than in their group or foster homes (Jacobs and Freundlich 2006).

Smith's policy and practice recommendations are detailed below.

THE SUPPORT NEEDS OF LESBIAN, GAY, BISEXUAL AND TRANS-GENDERED YOUNG PEOPLE (LGBT)

- Discrimination, safety issues and lack of support should be addressed within the foster care system by the recruitment of LGBT-friendly foster parents and staff, and mandatory training of foster parents group home staff, and child welfare professionals, on minority sexual orientation and gender identity.

- Staff of agencies providing after-care should be diverse in gender identity and sexual orientation to provide mentorship and role modelling; and provide safe environments for disclosure.

- Assessment processes should include consideration of LGBT identity and any consequences for young people – feelings of hopelessness, safety, suicide, exposure to harassment and discrimination, health conditions and practices, and risky sexual behaviour.

- Agencies and professionals should be knowledgeable about health education resources, community groups and support for LGBT young people.

(Source: Smith 2011, p.183)

Young offenders
Context
Official data on the offending rates of looked-after children in England were collected for the first time in 2000. Since that year it has shown that young people who are looked after have a higher than average likelihood of being involved in the youth justice system than other young people. Of the 30,230 children and young people looked after continuously for 12 months at the end of March 2011 who were aged between 10 and 17, 2210 (7.3%) had been convicted or subject to a final warning or reprimand during the year, compared with 3 per cent of all children. Offending was higher for young people aged 16 to 17 than those aged 13 to 15 and more frequent in boys (Department for Education 2010c, 2011b). There is also evidence that between a quarter and a half of young people in young offender institutions and prisons have been in care at some point previously in their lives (Blades *et al.* 2011). However, caution is necessary in making any causal connection, given the wide range of life course factors which may contribute to young people and adults being imprisoned.

Research findings: living in care
In their study of children's homes, Sinclair and Gibbs found that 40 per cent of young people with no cautions or convictions had one after six months of living in a children's home (Sinclair and Gibbs 1998). Also, research by Taylor suggests that for those who had already been involved in offending, care often had a negative effect, in particular escalating the criminal behaviour of young men (Taylor 2003). It has been suggested that young people in care may become criminalised because of their behaviour in care, particularly in children's homes, or due to their increased visibility or surveillance (NACRO 2005).

Qualitative research based on the views of 23 young people, aged 13–17, on whether being in care may contribute to the likelihood of them offending, found no coherent answers; 'this depended on individual experiences and pathways, before and after entering care' (Blades *et al.* 2011, p.2). However young people's views of what might contribute to offending included: loss of or infrequent contact with family and friends; poor relationships with carers and social workers; difficult relationships with peers and peer pressures; and types and numbers of placements. The opposite of each of these was seen by young people as 'protective' against offending and these form the basis of the researcher's recommendations for improving the quality of care (Blades *et al.* 2011). Research carried out by Schofield *et al.* (2012) into the relationship between looked-after children and offending, using a multi-method approach, has highlighted the importance of early entry to care and high-quality stable placements with good professional support, including education and health, to minimise the risk of offending behaviour. These are the foundations for promoting the resilience of young people from care. The study also showed that 'late entry to care can also reduce the risk of offending if it capitalises on the protective potential of relationships and involvement in constructive activities' (p.3). The research also identified as a 'serious risk factor... inappropriate criminalisation through police and court involvement, as a response to challenging behaviour or minor offences in their placement' (p.3).

Research findings: leaving care

Dixon *et al.*'s (2006) in-depth study of 101 young people included both baseline data on reported offending (in the 12 months in care prior to leaving care) and follow-up data (collected over nine months after leaving care). Leaving care worker assessments of the extent of offences committed by young people showed that:

- Over two-fifths of young people were assessed to have problems with offending at baseline and less than a third (27%) at follow-up.

- Nine per cent of young people were described as persistent offenders at baseline and 4 per cent at follow-up.

- Offences included assaults, fraud, criminal damage, drug use and dealing, alcohol-related violence and affray, burglary and theft, and several young people were involved in car theft and driving offences.

- Half of the young men in the study reported offending at baseline, twice as many as young women. By the follow-up the gap had widened to almost four times as many young men.

- There was an association between offending in care and committing offences after leaving care.

- Running away from care, truancy, poor education attainment and substance misuse were significantly related to offending.

- Those who had moved on from foster care were less likely to have offended at baseline than those accommodated in children's homes.

- Over a third of the sample had been the victim of crime during the follow-up period, most commonly reporting having been burgled, assaulted and being the victim of street robbery. Some young people were forced to leave their accommodation because of burglary.

- There was a link between offending over the follow-up period and a failure to achieve positive career outcomes – progressing well in education, training or employment.

- Those who had problems with offending were more likely to have moved accommodation more often than non-offenders after leaving care.

- There was an association between offending and poor mental well-being after leaving care.

- Young people who were being assisted by Youth Offending Teams, probation officers and leaving care workers were receiving more frequent support and contact than other young people in the study.

Additional support for care leavers in the youth justice system

The research findings discussed above suggest the need to consider offending behaviour in a wider context. Providing young people with stability in good-quality care, meeting their educational and well-being needs and supporting them on their pathways to adulthood may well prevent or reduce further offending. As detailed in the *Transitions Guidance* (see pp.41–44), young offenders from care may be supervised by Youth Offending Teams if they are under the age of 18 and the Probation Service after they reach 18 years of age. However it is important that there is a co-ordinated inter-agency response at strategic, operational and practice levels to ensure that:

- At arrest the young person has the support of an adult and access to a solicitor whilst at the police station.

- They have the same access to bail as other young people living at home through the provision of suitable accommodation and bail support programmes, as alternatives to secure accommodation.

• Information is shared between the personal adviser and the worker responsible for completing the criminal justice risk assessment and the pre-sentence report.

• When young people from care enter custody the pathway planning process continues and the young person is visited by their personal adviser on a regular basis and plans for resettlement on release.

• This includes plans for suitable accommodation, discharge arrangements, sources of support, assistance with education, employment and training, health care, financial support and clarity about the roles and responsibilities of leaving care, youth offending and probation staff.

• Where young people are supervised in the community by Youth Offending Teams or Probation, the contribution of the leaving care service is also clearly identified and co-ordinated.

Young people who misuse substances

Official data from England shows that 1960 young people (4.3%) who had been looked after continuously for at least 12 months had been identified as having a substance misuse problem during 2011 (Department for Education 2011b). Of these over half (56.6%) received an intervention for the problem but just over a third of young people (34.9%) refused the help that was offered. Substance abuse was more common among 16 to 17 year olds and among boys (Department for Education 2011b).

Research has revealed that compared with the general population, children and young people in care and young people leaving care have relatively high levels of tobacco, alcohol and drug use (Meltzer *et al.* 2003). Research based upon a survey of 400 young people (average age 15.4 years old), living in residential and foster care, also found that compared with the general population, young people in care have relatively high levels of illicit drug use, much higher proportions having used cannabis, solvents, amphetamines, ecstasy and cocaine (Newburn, Ward and Pearson 2002). The study showed that there was significantly higher use of crack and heroin among young people in care than in the general population and also more regular use of cannabis, cocaine, crack and heroin.

The same study also found that young people had often started using drugs early, which is correlated with problem drug-taking. However, drinking alcohol was a relatively infrequent activity. Many of the young people had experienced loss, bereavement and rejection and some of these young people had turned to drugs to compensate for these negative experiences and to combat depression (Newburn *et al.* 2002).

A survey of 200 young people (average age 18 years old) in the process of leaving care or home early, or having recently left care also found high levels of self-reported drug use compared with general population surveys (Ward, Henderson and Pearson 2003). But this was mainly cannabis use. Almost three-quarters (73%) have smoked it, one half (52%) in the last month, and a third (34%) reporting that they smoked daily. Fifteen per cent had used ecstasy and one-tenth had used cocaine within the last month. Little difference was found in drug use between young men and young women but young black people were less likely to use drugs (44% had not taken any drug) compared with 82 per cent of young white people who had. Among those of mixed parentage, 95 per cent had taken an illicit drug at some point in their lives. Two-thirds of the sample reported that they were daily cigarette smokers and one-third drank alcohol at least once a week (Ward *et al.* 2003).

Except for two groups, the qualitative interviews showed that lower levels of drug consumption were reported as young people assumed or approached independent living status. The groups being, first, those who went to live in hostels, and, second, those whose movement to independent living was premature or poorly planned. Parenthood and practical responsibilities, such as household management, when well planned as part of the care leaving transition encourage more stable lifestyles and reduce levels of drug use. The study also found that 'maturing out' of drug use occurs at a younger age for care leavers than that found within the general population (Ward *et al.* 2003).

Dixon *et al.*'s (2006) in-depth study of 101 care leavers also found high levels of substance abuse. Using a combined measure based on reports of both young people and their workers, the study showed that just under one in five young people had substance abuse problems before leaving care and this increased to around a third within nine months of leaving care. Assessment by leaving care workers identified just over a tenth as having moderate or serious problems before leaving care and this group increased to a fifth within months of leaving care.

There was little difference between males and females but this study also found that black young people were less likely to use drugs than white young people. The main routes into drug and alcohol use included teenage experimentation, peer pressure and a family history of substance misuse. The research also showed that young people with substance abuse problems tended to have more unstable early housing experiences, poor career outcomes and were more negative about their mental health and life in general.

The research also showed that although most of the young people received help, this was more likely general support than a specific intervention addressing their drug or alcohol problems. For those young people who did receive specialist help this included drug and addiction services provided by voluntary agencies or through the Youth Offending Team, plus additional support from leaving care services. There was also evidence of drug and alcohol problems impacting on other aspects of young people's lives – offending behaviour, relationship problems – resulting in a more holistic approach to support and including the involvement of other agencies, such as health and addiction agencies (Dixon *et al.* 2006).The additional support needs of substance-misusing young people include:

- Early identification of drug and substance misuse.

- Specialist help to assist young people by drug and addiction services.

- Recognition of the association between drug and alcohol problems and other dimensions of young people's lives and the need to tackle the underlying problems.

Summary points

- This chapter has identified the groups of young people who may require additional support – beyond that discussed in the earlier chapters – on their pathways to adulthood.

- For disabled young people this has included improving the quality of care, additional support during transition and learning from 'what works well' in moving from children's to adult services.

- The high rate of teenage parenthood among young people from care may be associated with negative birth family experiences and poor-quality care. Whatever the reasons it is important that young people receive both practical and personal support.

- Young people from black and minority ethnic groups, including those of mixed heritage, face many similar challenges to other young people leaving care on their pathways to adulthood, although there are differences between different ethnic groups. Their additional needs include a recognition of, and policy and practice responses to, identity issues, the impact of racism, building on positive family and community links, and having an ethnically diverse workforce.

- Working with unaccompanied asylum-seeking children means working with uncertainty while their asylum claim is being processed. Personal advisers have to identify and respond to the needs of young people making the transition from care to adulthood, having both a 'leaving care' and an 'immigration' status. The former will involve the personal adviser in needs assessment and pathway planning, taking into account the background of each young person, and any specialist needs arising from their circumstances. The latter will involve supporting young people during their asylum claim and its resolution.

- LGBT young people will be assisted by more recognition of their needs within the care system, including having more staff and carers diverse in gender identity and sexual orientation, more training of the workforce, and greater recognition of their needs in assessment processes and in providing ongoing support.

- Care leavers in the youth justice system will require a co-ordinated inter-agency response between leaving care services, Youth Offending Teams and Probation, in assisting them at arrest, on bail, on remand and on release from custody.

- For young people who misuse substances it is important that there is early identification of their behaviour whilst in care and they receive specialist help as well as support from leaving care services at that time and after they leave.

PART 3

CONCLUSION

Resilience is 'ordinary magic'.

(Ann S. Masten 2001)

Chapter 11

A Journey of Ideas

For an idea ever to be fashionable is ominous, since it must afterwards be always old-fashioned. (George Santayana 1913)

This book has explored the journey travelled by young people from leaving care to becoming adult. In this chapter I will reflect upon the ideas which have informed the earlier chapters and which arise from the research findings, upon which the main policy and practice implications are based. This will include discussion of social inclusion, universality and selectivity; participation; the life course; stability and attachment; and social transitions (Stein 2006c). These ideas will be drawn on in the concluding chapter to develop a theoretical framework for promoting the resilience of young people from care to adulthood (Stein 2005; 2008a).

Social inclusion, universality and selectivity

Young people leaving care are first and foremost young people, and as such their destiny is in part shaped by the opportunities, policies and attitudes that are common to all young people. As Chapter 2 has shown their high degree of vulnerability to unemployment during the 1980s, and from 2010, is an indicator of global economic, structural and social policy changes affecting young people more generally in society. Comprehensive universal policies on post-16 further and higher education, employment and training, income support, accommodation, health and well-being, which enhance all young people's opportunities on their pathways to adulthood, are the foundation stones upon which citizenship and social inclusion is built.

However, as the research reviewed in Part 2 of the book has shown, care leavers, as a group, are at high risk of social exclusion. They are more likely than young people who have not been in care to have poorer educational qualifications, lower levels of participation in post-16 further and higher education, to become homeless, as well as have higher levels of unemployment, physical and mental health problems, and offending behaviour. But, also, as detailed in Part 2 and discussed below, there are differences between care leavers in the progress they make, which, may be masked by a social exclusion perspective. In addition, as discussed in Chapter 10, specific groups of care leavers may need more support than other care leavers on their pathways to adulthood, including disabled young people, young parents, young people from minority ethnic backgrounds, unaccompanied asylum-seeking children and young people, LGBT young people, and, young offenders and substance abusers.

What this clearly shows is, first, care leavers as a group, and second, specific groups of care leavers, will often need selective or specialist services if they are to access and maximise their opportunities through universal services. Mendes, Johnson and Moslehuddin (2011) have proposed a 'social investment model' of support for care leavers, which 'requires policy makers to invest in affirmative action supports and programmes that can assist care leavers to overcome their early disadvantages, and effectively participate in mainstream social, economic and community activities' (p.54). And as research from Sweden shows, the needs of care leavers cannot be met by universal services alone (Höjer and Sjöblom 2011). Chapter 3 outlines the development of specialist leaving care services. It shows how these services have responded to the core needs of care leavers, for assistance on their pathways to adulthood, with accommodation, education, employment and training, finance, health and well-being and personal and social support.

However, at the same time, it is important that recognition is given to the balance to be struck between universal and selective services. For most care leavers it is not desirable for them to be trapped within specialist projects or provision, however well intentioned – the aim should be to provide the necessary additional support for young people to engage with universal services as soon as they are able, even when this may include a twin track approach. The 'corporate parenting case model' outlined in Chapter 3 appears organisationally well designed to achieve this balance through its formalised intra and inter-agency work set within clearly defined roles and responsibilities – and is well regarded by young people themselves. But, as detailed in Parts 1 and 2 of this book, there is evidence from both official data and research, including the views of young people, of unacceptable variation in the quality of leaving care services. An ongoing challenge of both selective and universal services is in reducing territorial injustices and improving the quality of leaving care services.

In response to this situation, a number of third sector organisations, including NCAS, A National Voice, The Care Leavers Foundation and the Princes Trust, are campaigning for central government departments to improve the support they offer to care leavers. The main proposal of their '*Access all Areas*' campaign is for central government departments to make a commitment to 'care proof' all government policies by assessing the impact they will have on the looked-after children and young people leaving care and those who support them: this would be co-ordinated and monitored through the setting up of across-departmental working group, each department producing an action plan through scrutiny of six areas:

1. *Explicit recognition* of the vulnerability of care leavers aged 18–25 and prioritisation of them in policy documents.

2. *Automatic entitlement* for care leavers aged 18–25 to provisions addressing the needs of vulnerable adults.

3. *Widespread* favourable interpretation of priority need and vulnerability for care leavers up to the age of 30 in all relevant policy areas where regulations and guidance have discretionary elements.

4. Create or maintain robust systems of *information and data sharing* between different government departments and local services.

5. Ensure *joint working and protocols* are in place between different government departments and local services and leaving care services.

6. *Responsive, personalised services* to care leavers.

(NCAS, 2012, P1)

However, tackling territorial injustices in order to reduce existing inequalities in the range and quality of leaving care services will require more recognition of the relationship between central government departments, local authorities and the providers of local services, as well as the relationship between universal and specialist services, as discussed above. One way of levelling up services would be to ensure formal links between 'good' and 'poor' services, with responsibilities for developing and reviewing action plans to bring about improvements. This process could also include sharing best practice in relation to specific groups of care leavers, discussed in Chapter 10, where there is evidence of service variation.

Participation

A focus on services, whether selective or universal, should not mask the importance of the quality of relationships – or how young people are involved individually in the decisions, and collectively in the policies, that affect their lives. The roots of young people's participation in England go back nearly 40 years, the Children Act 1975 marking the beginning of a journey that has seen major developments in law, policy and practice, both in the United Kingdom and internationally. And on this journey the rights movement of young people living in and leaving care in England have played a major part in bringing about change, and continue to do so, through the work of A National Voice (Stein 2011).

The arguments for young people's participation – to improve services; to improve decision making; to uphold children's rights; to fulfill legal responsibilities; to enhance the democratic process; and to promote children's protection – are increasingly recognised as the foundation of a rights-based approach to children's services at a local and national level.

In regard to the participation of young people living in and leaving care this is reflected at a policy level in the work of Children in Care Councils, the development of Pledges – or commitments to young people by local authorities to provide services, and the LILAC project (Leading Improvements for Looked-After Children) project, which involves young people as inspectors and assessors of services (Stein 2011). It is also reflected at a national level by the role of the Children's Commissioner and the Children's Rights Director for England, the latter's contribution including regular surveys of the views of young people living in and leaving care. NCAS has also introduced a Young Person's Benchmarking Forum.

In regard to practice, as detailed in Part 2 of this book, the involvement of young people is central to every stage: the making of care plans, the needs assessment and pathway planning process, preparation for leaving care and choice of accommodation, and the process of supporting young people on their pathways to adulthood. The strengthening of the role of Independent Reviewing Officers and the involvement of advocates in ensuring young people are prepared and ready, before they leave care, are discussed in Chapter 4. There is also research and practice evidence that young people whose transitions from care are successful are not only able to access more services but have more interactive relationships: they are able to *negotiate* good-quality accommodation, *engage* in education and employment and *participate* in community and leisure activities (Hart 1984; WMTD 2008).

But this is not to suggest there are no murky waters. Practitioners are confronted every day with difficult questions: who participates, and why, who doesn't, and why, how much does participation depend upon the age, the capability and choice of the young person, as well as the type of decisions to be taken, and how is a balance to be struck between contested professionally defined needs and young people's views?

The life course and outcomes

The research evidence reviewed in Part 2 of this book suggests that a life course approach can contribute to a greater understanding of young people's pathways to adulthood in three respects (Horrocks 2002). First, in that it sees young people's lives as an integrated whole as distinct from a series of separate cycles or developmental stages. This suggests that what happens to young people before entering care, whilst living in care and at the time of leaving care, should be seen as a cumulative process rather than self-contained experiences. Second, it recognises the inter-connected aspects of the individual life course – for example, as the chapters in Part 2 show, how young people's accommodation, career and health, and well-being pathways are often closely connected and reinforcing. Third, and central to the life course approach, is the inter-relationship between the personal biography and agency of young people and their social and economic contexts: this requires an understanding of how policies and interventions may either restrict or provide opportunities for young people leaving care to maximise their potential and, critically, how young people are involved and participate in shaping the services they receive, as discussed above.

In addition, ethnographic research using life course theory to explore the transitions of young people leaving care reminds us of the complexities in evaluating outcomes and the limitations of using single normative measures at fixed points in time – such as educational attainment at 16 years of age. There is a need to recognise the different starting points of young people, given the diversity of their social and family backgrounds; their care experiences; the dynamic nature of 'outcomes' for young people – they often change between 'official' measurement periods; the separation of outcome measures from each other, even though they are often closely inter-connected; and the normative assumptions often held about young people, whose lives have not been easy, achieving independence by 18 years of age. As has been suggested in Chapter 7, a more complex measure of progress made by young people is needed.

Stability in care and attachment

Part 2 of this book has highlighted young people's experience of instability and placement disruption, following their initial or later separation from their birth families, and the long shadow this may cast on young people's pathways to adulthood. A correlated review, of 92 international studies of looked-after children, identifies placement stability as a key mediator for a wide range of adult outcomes, including physical and mental health and employment (Jones *et al.* 2011). Studies carried out from 1980 show that between 30 and 40 per cent of young people had four or more moves and, within this group, between 6 and 10 per cent had a very large number of moves, as many as 10 or more (see Stein 2005 and Stein 2009a for a review of these studies). Attachment theory provides a framework for exploring young people's separation from their families and the circumstances surrounding it, including their patterns of attachment, care careers, placement disruption or stability, and the legacy of these experiences for their lives after care (Howe 2005; Schofield 2001; Schofield and Beek 2006).

As detailed in Part 2 of this book, the main implications are the need to provide young people with stable placements that can help them overcome their earlier problems and provide them with a strong emotional platform for their journey to adulthood. Young people need to be able to experience their carers as a secure base, to provide them with opportunities and active encouragement to explore and become confident in the adult world. Depending upon the age, development and individual circumstances of young people, including the quality of their family relationships, this may be achieved through compensatory attachments, or by providing young people with stability and continuity in their lives. As outlined in Chapter 4, there are good examples of formalising longer-term attachments with foster carers – by young people 'staying put' when they are settled with foster carers and a seamless transition between foster care and 'supported lodgings'.

Social transition

A consistent theme of this book, discussed in the Introduction and developed in Part 2, 'Pathways to Adulthood', is that a majority of young people leaving care move to independent living at between 16 and 18 years of age, whereas most of their peers remain at home well into their mid-to-late 20s. They are expected to undertake their journey to adulthood at a far younger age and in far less time than their peers: leaving foster care or their children's home and setting up a new home, often in a different area, and for some young people starting a family as well; leaving school and finding their way into further education, training or employment, or coping with unemployment. In short, their journey to adulthood is both accelerated and compressed. Also, for many of these young people, leaving care is often a final event – there is no option to return in times of difficulty.

However, after many years – research evidence dates back to 1986 (Stein and Carey 1986) – this is slowly beginning to change: more young people are leaving at 18 years of age and, as the examples given in Chapters 4 and 5 reveal, the law has been strengthened so that young people must have a greater say in when they leave care, and some young people are being given the opportunity to remain with their foster carers up to 21 years of age. But as young people in the general population are leaving care later a significant 'independence gap' still remains.

It is important that all young people from care whether living in foster care or children's homes are given the opportunity for gradual and extended transitions from care. The empirical testing of the 'focal model of adolescence', developed by Coleman, shows that having the opportunity to deal with inter-personal issues, spread over time, is how most young people cope successfully with the challenges of transition. Conversely, those young people who have to face a number of inter-personal issues at the same time are likely to experience significant problems of adjustment (Coleman and Hendry 1999). Research on transitions from care, drawing on an anthropological perspective complements focal theory and the arguments for giving young people from care normative experiences (Hart 1984).

Hart suggests that the process of social transition has traditionally included three distinct, but related stages: leaving or disengagement; transition itself; and integration into a new or different social state. In post (or late?) modern societies, providing more opportunities but also more risks, this process has become more extended and less structured for most young people, although the psychological 'activities' associated with the three stages still remain. As discussed above and in Part 2 of this book, for many young people leaving care there is the expectation of instant adulthood. They often miss out on the critical preparation stage, transition itself that gives young people an opportunity to 'space out', provides a time for freedom, exploration, reflection, risk taking and identity search.

For a majority of young people today this is gained through the experience of further and, especially, higher education but as Chapters 7 and 8 show, many care leavers, as a consequence of their pre-care and care experiences are unable to take advantage of these educational opportunities. Also, in the context of extended transitions, the family plays an increasing role in providing financial, practical and emotional support. But, as discussed in Chapter 5, for many care leavers their family relationships at this important time may be missing or problematic rather than supportive (Biehal and Wade 1996; Sinclair *et al.* 2005). In this context, as discussed in Part 2, the support provided by leaving care services and informal social networks is very important to young people.

Qualitative and ethnographic research has also increased our knowledge of the process of transition. Ward's work has shown that for many young people their past experience of placement disruption and discontinuity in their lives may represent a barrier to developing a sense of connectedness at the time of moving on and this may contribute to poor psychosocial outcomes (Ward 2011). A qualitative analysis of young people's accounts of their transition from care in Norway by Franson and Storro (2011) identifies three patterns of transition: breaking with the past after moving on; continuous change; and transition as a way of dealing with the risk of further problems in their lives. Qualitative research from Romania shows that young people often experience two different but inter-connected transitions – social and psychological – and they are expected to undertake the former (finding new accommodation, entering employment, making new friends), while, psychologically, they still need time to cope with ending relationships and separation (Dimma and Skehill 2011).

The main implications arising from these different but complementary perspectives on transition are: first, services should be organised to reflect the nature and timing of young people's transitions from care, more akin to normative transitions. This should include opportunities for all young people to remain in placements where they are settled – as is exemplified by the 'staying put' and 'going the extra mile' projects described in Chapter 5; and, second, the organisation and culture of services should recognise the need young people have for psychological space, in order to cope with changes over time. This should include recognition of the different stages of transitions, especially the significance of the middle stage, transition itself.

Summary points

- Young people will be assisted by a balance between universal and selective services. It is not desirable for young people to be trapped within specialist provision – the aim should be to support young people to engage with universal services as soon as they are able.

- Tackling territorial injustices in order to reduce existing inequalities in the range and quality of leaving care services will require recognition of the relationship between central government departments, local authorities and the providers of local services, as well as the relationship between universal and specialist services.

- Young people should be involved, individually, in all the decisions that shape their lives, and, collectively, in contributing to policy developments.

- A life course perspective recognises the connections between the different parts of young people's lives, both over time and in the challenges young people face on their pathways to adulthood.

- Stability in good-quality placements provides the emotional foundation for young people to achieve success on their pathways to adulthood.

- All young people should be provided with the opportunity for gradual and supported transitions from care, recognising the different stages of transition, including having the psychological space to cope with changes over time.

Chapter 12

Promoting Resilience from Care to Adulthood

Care, it's given me great opportunities...before I didn't have a clue what I wanted to do...now I know what direction I'm going in. At home my parents didn't care what I did.

This concluding chapter will explore how resilience can give coherence to the main themes, ideas and concepts which have informed the rationale of this book. It will begin by defining resilience and summarising the factors associated with promoting the resilience of young people from disadvantaged backgrounds. This will be followed by the application of 'resilience-promoting factors' to young people living in and leaving care, leading into a discussion of three main groups of young people leaving care: those successfully 'moving on' from care, those who get by, the 'survivors', and those who have the most difficulties, the 'strugglers'. This will provide the foundation for exploring how the main themes arising from the research studies, discussed in the preceding chapters, can contribute to the development of a resilience framework.

What is resilience?

Resilience can be defined as the quality that enables some young people to find fulfillment in their lives despite their disadvantaged backgrounds, the problems or adversity they may have undergone or the pressures they may experience. Resilience is about overcoming the odds, coping and recovery. But it is only relative to different ages and cultures, and risk experiences – relative resistance as distinct from invulnerability – and is likely to develop over time (Masten 2001, 2004; Rutter 1999). Also, finding resilience in young people does not require a competition. As Masten (2001) suggests, it is 'ordinary magic' – 'a common phenomenon that results from the operation of basic human adaption systems' (p.227).

Cavanan in his review of five recent definitions of resilience highlights the consistency running through them: 'while diverse, either implicit or explicit in all of them are concerns with development, adaption and outcomes, coping with threats and adversity, individual and environmental interaction, and supportive and undermining factors' (Cavanan 2008, p.2). As outlined in the introduction, this book adopts an ecological perspective on resilience and this is evident in the substantive narrative and the examples of good practice, focusing upon the quality of care, education, family and social networks, and how young people can be supported or hindered on their pathways to adulthood. An ecological perspective on resilience also recognises the relationship between individual development and social context, including the impact of structural inequalities and social policy responses, upon the lives of young people – as discussed in Chapter 2 and Part 2 of this book. Put simply, for many young people, changing the odds must go hand in hand with overcoming the odds.

Resilience-promoting factors

The resilience of young people from very disadvantaged family backgrounds has been found to be associated with a redeeming and warm relationship with at least one person in the family – or secure attachment to at least one unconditionally supportive parent or parent substitute; positive school experiences; feeling able to plan and be in control; being given the chance of a 'turning point', such as a new opportunity or break from a high-risk area; higher childhood IQ scores and lower rates of temperamental risk; and having positive peer influences (Rutter, Giller and Hagell 1998).

A research review of the international literature on resilience factors in relation to the key transitions made by children and young people during their whole life cycle has added to this picture (Newman and Blackburn 2002). As well as the factors identified above, the authors conclude that children and young people who are best equipped to overcome adversities will have: strong social support networks; a committed mentor or person from outside the family; a range of extra-curricular activities that promote the learning of competencies and emotional maturity; the capacity to re-frame adversities so that the beneficial as well as the damaging effects are recognised; the ability – or opportunity – to make a difference, for example, by helping others through volunteering, or undertaking part-time work; and exposure to challenging situations which provide opportunities to develop both problem-solving abilities and emotional coping skills (Newman and Blackburn 2002).

Promoting the resilience of young people living in and leaving care

As suggested at the beginning of Chapter 11, adopting a social exclusion framework may mask differences between different groups of care leavers, especially in relation to their progress and outcomes. By definition, social exclusion is about 'risk' factors and poor life chances. However, there is also a growing literature on 'looked-after' young people, adopting resilience as a central organising concept (Gilligan 2001; 2009; Newman 2004; Schofield 2001). How does this apply to young people leaving care?

The critical importance of providing young people with stability has been highlighted throughout Part 2 of this book and discussed in Chapter 11. Young people who experience stable placements providing good-quality care are more likely to succeed on their pathways to adulthood than those who have experienced further movement and disruption during their time in care. Stability has the potential to promote resilience in two respects. First, by providing the young person with a warm and redeeming relationship with a carer – or as discussed above, a compensatory secure attachment which may in itself reduce the likelihood of placement breakdown. Second, and not necessarily dependent on the first, stability may provide continuity of care in young people's lives, which may give them emotional security and contribute to positive educational and career outcomes.

Helping young people develop a positive sense of identity, including their self-knowledge, their self-esteem and self-efficacy, may also promote their resilience. And although not explicitly recognised as a variable in the research literature on resilience, identity could be seen as connected to, as well as a component of, key associations with resilience: feeling able to plan and be in control, and the capacity to re-frame adversities so that the beneficial as well as the damaging effects are recognised.

Helping care leavers develop a positive identity is linked to first, the quality of care and attachments experienced by looked-after young people – a significant resilience-promoting factor discussed above; second, to their knowledge and understanding of their background and personal history; third, to their experience of how other people perceive and respond to them; and finally, how they see themselves and the opportunities they have to influence and shape their own biography – as detailed in the discussion of participation in Chapter 11.

Having a positive experience of school, including achieving educational success, is associated with resilience among young people from disadvantaged family backgrounds and young people living in care. As detailed in Chapter 7, research evidence dating back to 1987, and the collection of national data from 1999, has shown that many children and young people who are looked after have lower levels of educational achievement than children in the general population. They are also more likely to have a statement of special educational needs, be excluded from, or miss school, and are less likely to go on to higher education.

The reasons for under-achievement are multi-faceted and include social disadvantage, poor birth parenting often contributing to social, emotional and behavioural problems, and the failure of care and education to compensate young people. As discussed in Chapter 7, a range of initiatives aimed at improving educational outcomes has been introduced since 1997 and these are having a positive effect on young people's educational experiences, although not, as yet, demonstrated outcomes. However, to focus exclusively on outcomes overlooks the evidence that many young people do make progress from very poor starting points and this should be recognised in official measures. The enduring nature of under-achievement – or the attainment gap – reflects the range and depth of aetiological factors and suggests that the promotion of resilience will require, first, a recognition of these factors and the wide-ranging responses this demands, and, second, a recognition of the progress made by individual young people.

Making progress and achieving success at school also lays the foundations for post-16 further and higher education, training and finding satisfying employment. Chapter 8 draws on the YiPPEE research project in identifying the 'facilitators' of young people from care continuing in post-16 education, focusing on the need for improvements to both care and education, including: placement stability; early support for catch-up learning; action-oriented Personal Education Plans; priority given to education by social workers and carers; individual tutoring to compensate for gaps in schooling; support from family, carers and professionals; financial resources and practical help; sympathetic schools; clear protocols agreed with colleges and higher education institutions; staying in placement after 18; and the leaving care team promoting education over employment, and including an education specialist.

Chapter 8 also provides examples of improving the employment opportunities of young people from care from the NCAS's From Care2Work project. Their main messages from the first three years of running the project highlight the contribution of corporate parenting, a partnership approach, raising aspirations and supporting the journey to work.

School or care itself may also provide turning points, opening the door for participation in a range of leisure or extra-curricular activities that may lead to new friends and opportunities, including the learning of competencies and the development of emotional maturity – and thus promote their resilience. Indeed, resilient young people have often been able to turn their negative experiences at home, or in care, into opportunities, with the help of others.

As detailed in Chapter 3, preparation for leaving care may also provide young people with opportunities for planning, problem solving and the learning of new competencies – all resilience-promoting factors. This may include the development of self-care skills – personal hygiene, diet and health, including sexual health; practical skills – budgeting, shopping cooking and cleaning; and inter-personal skills – managing a range of formal and informal relationships. Preparation should be holistic in approach, attaching equal importance to practical, emotional and interpersonal skills for young people.

Being in good health and having a positive sense of well-being is another way of framing resilience. As Chapter 9 details, many children and young people enter care with both physical and mental health problems and these may increase when young people are coping with the demands of leaving care. On entry to care young people should have a comprehensive assessment of their needs, the provision of stable high-quality placements, which may include 'treatment foster care', and other therapeutic interventions to address their social, emotional or behavioural needs. As discussed in Chapter 11, the psychological demands of accelerated and compressed transitions should be replaced by providing all young people with the opportunities for more gradual transitions from care, ongoing support into adulthood by leaving care services and by maintaining positive family and kinship networks. As detailed in Chapter 10, specific groups of care leavers may benefit from additional support services to promote their resilience on their pathways to adulthood.

Groups of young people

Drawing on the research findings discussed above, including studies carried out between 1980 and 2012, suggests that young people may broadly fall into one of three groups, those 'moving on' from care, 'survivors' and those who are 'strugglers'. Identifying these groups provides one way of connecting the generality of the research findings discussed in this book to young people's lives, including the implications for promoting their resilience. Although they are not set groups, young people may move between them, over time, or as their circumstances or the support they receive changes.

Moving on

> I feel more of a person now that I'm on my own and I ain't got to go and ask permission for this and that... I feel like myself now, more normal.

The first group, those young people successfully 'moving on' from care, are likely to have had stability and continuity in their lives, including a secure attachment relationship; made sense of their family relationships so they could psychologically move on from them; and have achieved some educational success before leaving care. Their preparation had been gradual, they had left care later and their moving on was likely to have been planned. They were able to move from 'selective' to 'universal' services. Participating in further or higher education, having a job they liked, finding a partner, or being a parent themselves, played a significant part in 'feeling normal', or developing a post-care identity.

The 'moving on' group welcomed the challenge of independent living and gaining more control over their lives. They saw this as improving their confidence and self-esteem. In general, their resilience had been enhanced by their experiences of living in, leaving and after care. They had been able to make good use of the help they have been offered, often maintaining contact and support from former carers and having supportive social networks.

Survivors

> I've become more independent...more tough... I know more about
> the world.

The second group, the 'survivors', had experienced more instability, movement and disruption while living in care than the 'moving on' group. They were also likely to leave care younger, with few or no qualifications, and often following a breakdown in foster care or a sudden exit from their children's home. They were likely to experience further movement and problems after leaving care, including periods of homelessness, low-paid casual or short-term, unfulfilling work and unemployment. They were also likely to experience problems in their personal and professional relationships through patterns of detachment and dependency.

Many in this group saw themselves as 'more tough', as having done things 'off my own back' and as 'survivors' since leaving care. They believed that the many problems they had faced, and often were still coping with, had made them more grown-up and self-reliant – although their view of themselves as independent was often contradicted by the reality of high degrees of agency dependency for assistance with accommodation, money and personal problems. As research from the Unites States found, their view of themselves as self-reliant – 'what doesn't kill you makes you stronger' (a young person leaving care, citing Nietzsche) – could also restrict and damage their informal social networks and their help-seeking relationships (Samuels and Pryce 2008, p.1208).

The research evidence discussed in this book shows that what made the difference to their lives, or promoted their resilience, was the professional support they received on their pathways to adulthood. Specialist leaving care workers and personal advisers could assist these young people. Also, mentoring, including mentoring by ex-care young people (or peer mentoring), may assist young people during their journey to independence, and offer them a different type of relationship from professional support or troubled family relationships. Helping young people in finding and maintaining their accommodation can be critical to their mental health and well-being. Families, including kin and friends may also help, where these relationships can build on earlier positive experiences, but for some young people returning to them may prove very problematic. Overall, and over time, some combination of professional and personal support networks could help them overcome their very poor starting points, and successfully move on.

Strugglers

> I hate being like I am… I don't care about myself, so why should I care about other people.

The third group of care leavers, the strugglers, was the most disadvantaged. They had the most damaging pre-care family experiences, often including severe maltreatment and, in the main, care was unable to compensate them, or to help them overcome their past difficulties. Their lives in care were likely to include many further placement moves, the largest number of moves in the different research studies cited above, and the associated disruption to their lives, especially in relation to their personal relationships and education.

They were also likely to have a cluster of difficulties while in care that often began earlier, including social, emotional and behavioural difficulties, problems at school and getting into trouble. They were the least likely to have a redeeming relationship with a family member or carer, and were likely to leave care younger, following a placement breakdown. At the time of leaving care their life chances were very poor indeed. After leaving care they were likely to be unemployed, become homeless and have great difficulties in maintaining their accommodation. They were also highly likely to be lonely, isolated and have mental health problems, often being defined by projects as young people with very complex needs. Support by leaving care services was not always able to help them overcome their very poor starting points and they also lacked or alienated professional and personal support. But it was important to these young people that somebody was there for them and they could benefit from the specialist support services discussed in Chapters 9 and 10.

Promoting resilience across the life course – an international perspective

Table 12.1 brings together the main themes identified in this chapter. It also provides a framework for thinking about leaving care more internationally, as the underpinning ideas – resilience, attachment, social transition, participation, universality and selectivity – have relevance to young people leaving care and becoming adult wherever they are living.

It is only during the last decade that research has contributed to a greater understanding of young people leaving care, internationally. Growing international evidence of social exclusion – the poor outcomes for children in care and the long shadow they cast on young people's journey to adulthood – led in 2003 to the setting up of the Transitions from Care to Adulthood International Research Group (INTRAC), bringing together, for the first time, researchers from Europe, the Middle East, Australia, Canada and the United States.

The work of the group resulted in an initial mapping publication which included 16 country chapters using a standardised framework (key contextual data; case examples; types of welfare regimes; legal and policy context; use of secondary data; and research findings) and four thematic chapters (global issues; legal and policy frameworks; the use of secondary data; and messages from research). The volume concluded by recognising the need to build upon these foundations through further exploration of local, national and global processes (Stein and Munro 2008).

In 2010, in response to limited knowledge of young people's transitions to adulthood in eastern European and central Asian post-communist societies, the child care charity, SOS Children's Villages carried out a baseline survey of 12 countries, adopting the INTRAC framework detailed above (Lerch with Stein 2010). Further research carried out by members of INTRAC has resulted in a special edition of *Children and Youth Services Review* (Stein, Ward and Courtney 2011).

However as Pinkerton has suggested, although progress has been made since 2003 – and there is evidence of cultural diversity with the INTRAC countries (Anghel 2011; Ibrahim and Howe 2011) – we are still a long way from having a global perspective – 'there is no readily available material on leaving care in Africa, China, India and South America' (p.2412). In addition, a survey of 15 countries shows that there is limited engagement with understanding and promoting the needs of care leavers under the United Nation Convention on the Rights of the Child (UNCRC), unless a government is committed to developing its own legislation. The authors suggest that new UNCRC *Guidelines for the Alternative Care of Children* may result in leaving care receiving a higher priority (Munro *et al.* 2012).

Table 12.1: Promoting resilience across the life course

Resilience-promoting factors	Selective services	Universal services
Living in care		
Attachment, stability, positive sense of identity and well-being	Good-quality placements, 'authoritative parenting'	Parenting education
Positive experience of school	Assessment Specialist compensatory help – education, health, well-being	Education Health services
Turning points	New experiences	Youth, leisure
Planning, problem solving, learning	Holistic preparation Participation	Participation
Transitions from care		
Transition as a normative process	Staying put in placements when settled	Continuity of services
Opportunities and space to focus and deal with issues over time	Pathway planning and support for accommodation, careers, health and well-being	Post-16 education, employment, training, housing services, health services
	Financial assistance	Benefits agency
Social networks	Maintain networks	Youth, leisure Explore new networks
Care to adulthood		
Gaining more control over lives and challenge of independent living	Move on from placement when ready	Housing options
Career satisfaction, education, employment, parenthood	Continue pathway planning and financial support	Higher education Careers
Positive attachment to partner, partner's family, birth family member, former carer	Contact with former carers	
Social networks	Friendships from care	Networks from education, work, leisure
Make sense of negative birth family relationships, so can psychologically move on	Referral for counselling	Health services

As a way forward, Pinkerton has suggested two directions for research. First, a three-domain model for making international comparisons: a macro domain referring to large-scale international processes directly affecting nation states; a mezzo domain where relationships between the national state, welfare regimes and social professions are played out; and the micro domain which focuses on everyday practice (Pinkerton 2008). Second, he proposes a 'globalised social ecology of care leaving' (p.2414) (Pinkerton 2011). This brings together the concepts of resilience and social capital and their potential benefits to young people leaving care within a social ecology of support.

Finally, a connecting theme arising from the body of research findings discussed in this book is that leaving care should be at one with a common journey, from being a young person to becoming an adult. Those young people who experience such a common journey, assisted by universal and selective services matched to their needs, are the most likely to find fulfillment in their careers and personal lives, and overcome some of the damaging consequences of familial problems, abuse or neglect. By experiencing good-quality care, being well prepared and being supported on their pathways to adulthood, they are able to become more independent, not in an emotionally isolated or detached way, but by 'moving on' successfully from care, and thus achieve an 'ordinary' or 'common' identity.

Needs Assessment and Content of Pathway Plans for Relevant and Former Relevant Children

	Dimensions of need	Plan to include
1.	*Health and development*	• Use of primary healthcare services. • Arrangements for the young person's medical and dental care according to their needs making reference to the health plan established within the care plan in place when the young person was looked after. • Access to specialist health and therapeutic services. • Arrangements so that the young person understands the actions they can take to maintain a healthy lifestyle. • Opportunities to enjoy and achieve and take part in positive leisure activities.
2.	*Education, training and employment*	• Statement of the young person's aspirations and career ambitions, and actions and support to achieve this. • Access to careers advice. • Education objectives and support – continue to use the young person's Personal Education Plan. • Arrangements to support the young person in further education and/or higher education. • Support to enable suitably qualified young people to enter apprenticeships, make applications to university or gain necessary qualifications. • Arrangements for work experience, career mentoring or pathways into employment, etc.
3.	*Emotional and behavioural development*	• How the authority will assist the young person to develop self-esteem and maintain positive attachments. • Does the young person display self-esteem, resilience and confidence? • Assessment of their capacity to empathise with others, reason and take appropriate responsibility for their own actions.

Cont.

		• Capacity to make attachments and appropriate relationships; show appropriate emotion; adapt to change; manage stress; and show self-control and appropriate self-awareness.
4.	*Identity*	• How the authority intends to meet any of the young person's needs arising from their ethnicity, religious persuasion, sexual orientation. • How does the young person understand their identity stemming from being a child in care and a care leaver? • How the authority will assist the young person to obtain key documents linked to confirming their age and identity.
5.	*Family and social relationships*	• Assessment of the young person's relationship with their parents and wider family. • Contact with family – carried across from care plan. • Young person's relationship with peers, friendship network and significant adults. Strategy to improve any negative features of these relationships. • How all these relationships will contribute to the young person making a successful transition to adulthood and how they will assist with integration into the community that they identify with.
6.	*Practical and other skills necessary for independent living*	• The young person is adequately prepared with the full range of practical skills they will need to manage the next planned move towards greater independence. • The young person is prepared for taking greater responsibility as they are expected to manage more independently.
7.	*Financial arrangements*	• Assessment of care leaver's financial needs and their financial capability. Does the young person have a bank account, national insurance number, and appreciate the value of regular saving, etc? Do they have access to financial support and adequate income to meet necessary expenses? • Pathway plan must include a statement of how the authority proposes to maintain a relevant child, the arrangements in place for the young person to receive financial support and contingency plans. • Statement of financial assistance to be provided to a former relevant child.
8.	*(Suitability of) Accommodation*	• An assessment of the quality of accommodation where the young person is living/any accommodation under consideration for them to live in. • How far is this suitable to the full range of the young person's needs? • What steps might need to be taken to improve it? (Schedule 2 of the *Care Leavers Regulations*)

Source: *Transitions Guidance* (Department for Education 2010a, p.17)

Planning for Education, Training and Careers

- Young people require a great deal of stability when undertaking education activities. Early planning is vital when they are considering attending university, particularly where they are moving away from their home area and therefore placement arrangements from their 18th birthday to the point they commence higher education courses must be addressed and agreed well in advance of their 18th birthday. Arrangements may need to be made for young people to remain with the families who have fostered them beyond their 18th birthday; and plans need to be made for the vacation breaks (5.6).

- Young people will need to know what practical and financial support they will receive from their local authorities and therefore the authority should have a written policy they give to looked-after children and care leavers detailing the financial support that they will receive when they participate in any further or higher education. Information about the financial support each care leaver can expect, as set out in their responsible authority's policy, should be complemented by information setting out what support the young person will be entitled to from the universal student funding sources (5.7).

- Pathway planning must continue for all former relevant children in any continuing education or training. As many young people at university will be living away from their home area and previous carers and support networks, the pathway plan for each individual child must set out what practical support they can expect from their local authority. These arrangements should include the level and frequency of contact with their personal adviser. The plan should specify arrangements for meeting the young person in the area where they are attending university. It may be desirable to involve one specified member of university staff (perhaps the care leaver's personal tutor) in some of these meetings, so that the higher education institution is firmly engaged with the pathway planning process, and to make sure that the care leavers concerned are getting every possible support as they study for their degree and achieve their potential (5.8).

- Pathway plans must set out accommodation arrangements, including financial arrangements during term time, short vacations and the long vacation during the summer. Where young people are unable to return to their former placements then they must be provided with a stable alternative accommodation best suited to their personal circumstances. For some young people this may involve returning to accommodation in their responsible authority's area; others may prefer to remain in the area of their university and many universities now provide 52-week accommodation. Regardless of which option is required, early planning is essential (5.9).

- Where young people are continuing with an education or training course beyond their 21st birthday, the practical and financial support being provided must continue to be set out in their pathway plan (5.10).

- Given the specialist knowledge that is likely to be needed to maximise support for care leavers at university, local authorities may wish to consider developing a dedicated personal adviser role for this group of young people. The role could be used to provide the expertise and knowledge needed to both make sure that young people are visited by their responsible authority and that they receive appropriate support and academic advice from the higher education institution that they have joined (5.11).

- Local authorities should make sure that they have policies and processes in place to support every care leaver undertaking apprenticeships, traineeships, vocational courses or employment. These policies will need to take into account the universal financial support that the young person will receive and allow for the local authority to assess whether the young person requires any additional financial contribution from the authority, so that they can benefit fully from taking part in a broad range of training opportunities or employment (5.4).

- Joint work with Integrated Youth Services/Connexions and Careers Advisers is vital so that responsible authorities make sure that young people are fully aware of the options and entitlements available to them. Local authorities should use career planning tools to inform young people's pathway plans (5.5).

- Authorities should work with their partners to address the employment, education and training needs of care leavers in their areas. Pathway plans should outline how the local authority will improve the employability of their care leavers. They should ensure that care leavers are aware of and get access to work experience, apprenticeships and other training and employment opportunities (5.15).

Source: *Transitions Guidance* (Chapter 5, pp.31–33)

Clarke, J. (1996) 'After Social Work.' In N. Parton (ed.) *Social Theory, Social Change and Social Work.* London: Routledge.

Clayden, J. and Stein, M. (2005) *Mentoring Young People Leaving Care, Someone for Me.* York: Joseph Rowntree Foundation.

Coleman, J.C. and Hendry, L. (1999) *The Nature of Adolescence.* London: Routledge.

Collins, M.E. (2001) 'Transition to adulthood for vulnerable youths: a review of research and implications for policy.' *Social Service Review,* 75, 2, 271–291.

Colton, M (2002) 'Factors associated with abuse in residential child care institutions.' *Children and Society,* 16, 1, 33–44.

Consumer Focus (2011) *Care Leavers' Perspectives on Public Services, Exploring Barriers for Care Leavers Using Public Services in England.* London: Community Focus.

Courtney, M.E. and Dworsky, A. (2006) 'Early outcomes for young adults transitioning from out-of-home care in the USA.' *Child and Family Social Work,* 11, 3, 209–219.

Courtney, M.E., Lee, J.A. and Perez, A. (2011) 'Receipt of help acquiring life skills and predictors of help receipt among current and former foster youth.' *Children and Youth Services Review,* 33, 12, 2242–2451.

Davies, C. and Ward, H. (2011) *Safeguarding Children Across Services: Messages from Research.* London: Jessica Kingsley Publishers.

Department for Children, Schools and Families (2009) *Care Matters: Ministerial Stocktake Report 2009.* London: Department for Children, Schools and Families.

Department for Children, Schools and Families (2010) *Promoting the Emotional Health of Children and Young People, Guidance for Children's Trust partnerships, Including How to Deliver NI 50.* London: Department for Children, Schools and Families.

Department for Children, Schools and Families and Communities and Local Government (2010) *Provision of Accommodation for 16 and 17 Year Old Young People who may be Homeless and/or Require Accommodation.* London: Department for Children, Schools and Families and CLG.

Department for Children, Schools and Families and Department of Health (2009) *Statutory Guidance on Promoting the Health and Well-being of Looked After Children.* London: Department for Children, Schools and Families and Department of Health.

Department for Education (2010a) *The Children Act 1989 Guidance and Regulations Volume 3: Planning Transition to Adulthood for Care Leavers.* London: Department for Education.

Department for Education (2010b) *Children Act 1989 Guidance and Regulations, Volume 2, The Care Planning, Placements and Case Review (England) Regulations 2010* and the *Care Planning, Placements and Case Review Regulations 2010 Statutory Guidance.* London: Department for Education.

Department for Education (2010c) *Outcomes for Children Looked After by Local Authorities in England, as at 31 March 2010* (statistical first release 16/12/2010). London: Department for Education.

Department for Education (2010d) *Children Looked After in England (Including Adoption and Care Leavers) Year Ending 31 March 2010* (statistical first release 30/9/2010). London: Department for Education.

Department for Education (2011a) *Children Looked After in England (Including Adoption and Care Leavers) Year Ending 31 March 2011* (statistical first release 28/9/2011). London: Department for Education.

Department for Education (2011b) *Outcomes for Children Looked After by Local Authorities In England, as at 31 March 2011* (statistical first release 14 December 2011). London: Department for Education.

Department for Education and Skills (2003) *Every Child Matters.* London: HMSO.

Department for Education and Skills (2004) *Every Child Matters: Change for Children.* London: HMSO.

Department for Education and Skills (2005) *Youth Matters.* London: HMSO.

Department for Education and Skills (2006) *Care Matters: Transforming the Lives of Children and Young People in Care.* London: HMSO.

Department for Education and Skills (2007) *Care Matters: Time for Change.* London: HMSO.

Department of the Environment (1981) *Single and Homeless.* London: HMSO.

Department of Health (1997) *'When Leaving Home is Also Leaving Care': An Inspection of Services for Young People Leaving Care.* Social Services Inspectorate. London: Department of Health.

Department of Health (1998) *Quality Protects: Framework for Action.* London: Department of Health.

Department of Health (1999) *Me, Survive, Out There? New Arrangements for Young People Living in and Leaving Care.* London: Department of Health.

Department of Health (2000) Local Authority Circular, LAC (2000) 15.

Department of Health (2001) *Children (Leaving Care) Act 2000: Regulations and Guidance.* London: Department of Health.

Department of Health (2003) *Guidance on Accommodating Children in Need and Their Families.* LAC 13. London: Department of Health.

Del Valle, G., Lázaro-Visa, S., López, M. and Bravo, A. (2011) 'Leaving family care: transitions to adulthood from kinship care.' *Children and Youth Services Review*, 33, 2475–2481.

Dickson, K., Sutcliffe, K., Gough, D. and Statham, J. (2010) *Improving the Emotional and Behavioural Health of Looked-After Children and Young People.* Vulnerable Children Knowledge Review 2. London: C4EO.

Dimma, G. and Skehill, C. (2011) 'Making sense of leaving care: the contribution of Bridges model of transition to understanding the psycho-social process.' *Children and Youth Services Review*, 33, 12, 2532–2539.

Dixon, J. (2008) 'Young people leaving care: health, well-being and outcomes.' *Child and Family Social Work*, 13, 2, 207–217.

Dixon, J., Lee, J., Wade, J., Byford, S., Weatherley, H. and Lee, J. (2006) *Young People Leaving Care: an Evaluation of Costs and Outcomes.* Final Report to the Department for Education. York: Social Policy Research Unity, University of York.

Dixon, J. and Stein, M. (2005) *Leaving Care, Through Care and Aftercare in Scotland.* London: Jessica Kingsley Publishers.

Donkoh, C., Underhill, K. and Montgomery, P. (2006) *Independent Living Programmes for Improving Outcomes for Young People Leaving the Care System* (Campbell Systematic Reviews). Oslo: Campbell Collaboration.

Donzelot, J. (1980) *The Policing of Families.* London: Hutchinson.

Farmer, E. and Moyers, S. (2008) *Kinship Care, Fostering Effective Family and Friends Placements.* London: Jessica Kingsley Publishers.

First Key (1987) *A Study of Black Young People Leaving Care.* Leeds: First Key.

First Key (1992) *A Survey of Local Authority Provision for Young People Leaving Care.* Leeds: First Key.

Flynn, J.R. and Tessier, G.N. (2011) 'Promotive and risk factors as concurrent predictors of educational outcomes in supported transitional living: extended care and maintenance in Ontario.' *Children and Youth Services Review*, 33, 2498–2503.

Ford, T., Vostanis, P., Meltzer, H. and Goodman, R. (2007) 'Psychiatric disorder among British children looked after by local authorities: comparison with children living in private households.' *British Journal of Psychiatry*, 19, 319–325.

Fostering Network (2011) *More than a Room.* Conference Report. London: The Fostering Network.

Foyer Federation (2011) *Identification of Good Practice in Enhanced Housing Support for Teenage Parents: a Report by the Foyer Federation.* London: The Foyer Federation.

Franson, E. and Storro, J. (2011) 'Dealing with the past in the transition from care: a post-structural analysis of young people's accounts.' *Children and Youth Services Review*, 33, 12, 2519–2525.

Garnett, L. (1992) *Leaving Care and After.* London: National Children's Bureau.

Georgiades, S.D. (2005) 'A multi-outcome evaluation of an independent living program.' *Child and Adolescent Social Work Journal*, 22, 5–6, 417–439.

Giddens, A. (1991) *Modernity and Self-identity: Self and Society in the Late Modern Age.* Cambridge: Polity Press.

Gilligan, R. (2001) *Promoting Resilience: a Resource Guide on Working with Children in the Care System.* London: BAAF.

Gilligan, R. (2009) *Promoting Resilience: Supporting Children and Young People who are in Care, Adopted, or in Need.* London: BAAF.

Glover, J. and Clewett, N. (2011) *No Fixed Abode: the Housing Struggle for Young People Leaving Care in England.* Barkingside: Barnardo's.

Godek, S. (1976) *Leaving Care.* Barkingside: Barnardo's.

Gordon, D., Parker, R. and Loughran, F. (2000) *Disabled Children in Britain: a Re-analysis of the OPCS Disability Survey.* London: HMSO.

Hai, N. and Williams, A. (2004) *Implementing the Children (Leaving Care) Act 2000, The Experience of Eight London Boroughs.* London: NCB.

Hannon, C., Wood, C. and Bazalgette, L. (2010) *In Loco Parentis.* London: Demos.

Harder, T.A., Knorth, E.J. and Kalverboer, M.E. (2011) 'Transition secured? A follow-up study of adolescents who have left secure residential care.' *Children and Youth Services Review,* 33, 12, 2482–2488.

Harris, J., Rabiee, P. and Priestley, M. (2002) 'Enabled by the Act? The Reframing of Aftercare Services for Young Disabled.' In A. Wheal (ed.) *The RHP Companion to Leaving Care.* Lyme Regis: Russell House Publishing.

Hart, A. (1984) 'Resources for Transitions from Care.' In *Leaving Care – Where? Conference Report.* London: National Association of Young People in Care.

Heywood, J. (1978) *Children in Care.* London: Routledge.

HM Government (2011a) *Consultation on Preventing Suicide in England: a Cross-Government Strategy to Save Lives.* London: HM Government.

HM Government (2011b) *Safeguarding Children Who May Have Been Trafficked: Practice Guidance.* London: Department for Education, Home Office.

HM Inspectorate of Prisons (2011a) *The Care of Looked After Children in Custody: a Short Thematic Review.* London: HM Inspector of Prisons.

HM Inspectorate of Prisons (2011b) *Resettlement Provision for Children and Young People, Accommodation and Education, Training and Employment.* London: HM Inspector of Prisons.

Hodes, M., Jagdev, D., Chandra, N. and Cunniff, A. (2008) 'Risk and resilience for psychological distress amongst unaccompanied asylum seeking adolescents.' *Child Psychology and Psychiatry,* 49, 7, 723–732.

Höjer, I., Johansson, H., Hill, M., Cameron, C. and Jackson, S. (2008) *The Educational Pathways of Young People From a Public Care Background in Five EU Countries.* London: University of London, Institute of Education, Thomas Coram Research Unit.

Höjer, I. and Sjöblom, Y. (2011) 'Procedures when young people leave care – views of 111 Swedish social services managers.' *Children and Youth Services Review,* 33, 12, 2452–2460.

Horrocks, C. (2002) 'Using life course theory to explore the social and developmental pathways of young people leaving care.' *Journal of Youth Studies,* 5, 3, 325–335.

House of Commons (1968) *Report of the Committee on Local Authority and Allied Personal Social Services.* London: HMSO.

House of Commons (1984) *Second Report from the Social Services Committee, Children in Care.* London: HMSO.

House of Commons (2000) *Report of the Tribunal of Inquiry into the Abuse of Children in Care in the Former County Council Areas of Gwynedd and Cllwyd Since 1974: Lost in Care,* London: HMSO.

House of Commons (2011) *Looked After Children: Further Government Response to the Third Report from the Children, Schools and Families Committee, Session 2008–09, Fifth Special Report of Session 2010–11.* London: HMSO.

Howe, D. (1995) *Attachment Theory for Social Work Practice.* London: Macmillan.

Howe, D. (2005) *Child Abuse and Neglect: Attachment, Development and Intervention.* Basingstoke: Palgrave Macmillan.

Ibrahim, R.W. and Howe, D. (2011) 'The experience of Jordanian care leavers making the transition from residential care to adulthood: the influence of a patriarchal and collectivist culture.' *Children and Youth Services Review*, 33, 12, 2469–2474.

Iglehart, A.P. (ed.) (2004) 'Kinship foster care: filling the gaps in theory, practice and research' (special issue).' *Children and Youth Services Review*, 26, 7, 613–686.

Jackson, S. (1987) *The Education of Children in Care*. Bristol: School of Applied Social Studies, University of Bristol.

Jackson, S. (2002) 'Promoting stability and continuity of care away from home.' In D. McNeish, T. Newman and H. Roberts (eds) *What Works For Children?* Buckingham: Open University Press.

Jackson, S., Ajayi, S. and Quigley, M. (2005) *Going to University from Care*. London: Institute of Education.

Jackson, S., Cameron, C., Hollingworth, K. and Hauri, H. (2011) 'England.' In S. Jackson and C. Cameron (eds) *Final Report of the YiPPEE Project, WP12, Young People From a Public Care Background: Pathways to Further and Higher Education in Five European Countries*. London: Thomas Coram Research Unit, Institute of Education, University of London.

Jackson, S. and Sachdev, D. (2001) *Better Education, Better Futures: Research, Practice and the Views of Young People in Public Care*. Ilford: Barnardo's.

Jackson, S. and Thomas, N. (2001) *What Works in Creating Stability for Looked After Children*. Ilford: Barnardo's.

Jacobs, J. and Freundlich, M. (2006) 'Achieving permanency for LGBTQ youth in care.' *Child Welfare*, 85, 2, 299–316.

Jones, R., Everson-Hock, E.S., Papaioannou, D. *et al.* (2011) 'Factors associated with outcomes for looked after children and young people; a correlates review of the literature.' *Child: Care, Health and Development*, 37, 5, 613–622.

Kahan, B. (1976) *Growing Up in Care*. Oxford: Blackwell.

Kiernan, K. (1992) 'The impact of family disruption in childhood on transitions made in young adult life.' *Population Studies*, 46, 213–234.

Kohli, R. and Mather, R. (2003) 'Promoting psychosocial well-being in unaccompanied young asylum seekers.' *Child and Family Social Work*, 8, 3, 201–212.

Leonard, C. (2011) *Care Leavers in Further Education – the Lost Cohort*. Research Report for Aimhigher West Area Partnership. Bristol: Aimhigher.

Lerch, V. with Stein, M. (eds) (2010) *Ageing Out of Care: From Care to Adulthood in European and Central Asian Societies*. Innsbruck: SOS Children's Villages.

Lupton, C. (1985) *Moving Out*. Portsmouth: Portsmouth Polytechnic.

Malek, M. (2011) *Enjoy, Achieve and Be Healthy, the Mental Health of Black and Minority Ethnic Children and Young People*. London: The Afiya Trust.

Malek, M. and Joughlin, C. (2004) *Mental Health Services for Minority Ethnic Children and Adolescents*. London: Jessica Kingsley Publishers.

Marsh, P. and Peel, M. (1999) *Leaving Care in Partnership: Family Involvement with Care Leavers*. London: HMSO.

Masten, A.S. (2001) 'Ordinary magic: resilience processes in development.' *American Psychologist*, 56, 227–238.

Masten, A.S. (2004) 'Regulatory processes, risk and resilience in adolescence.' *American Psychologist*, 56, 227–238.

McAuley, C. (2005) *Pathways and Outcomes: a Ten Year Follow Up Study of Children who have Experienced Care*. Belfast: Department of Health, Social Services and Public Safety. Available at www.equality.nisra.gov.uk/pathways.pdf, accessed on 5 March 2012.

McBriar, N., Noade, L. and Ringland, B. (2001) 'First evaluation of the Down Lisburn Trust befriending scheme for young people leaving care.' *Child Care in Practice*, 7, 2, 164–174.

McCrea, R. (2008) *Evaluation of the Former Foster Care Scheme 'Fostering a Better Future for Young People'* (Leaving Care Implementation Project). Belfast: The Fostering Network.

McDowell, J. (2011) *Transitioning from Care in Australia: an Evaluation of Create's 'What's the Plan?'* *Campaign*. Create Report Card 2011. Sydney: Create Foundation.

McKelvey, R.S. and Webb, J.A. (1995) 'Unaccompanied status as a risk factor in Vietnamese Amerasians.' *Social Science and Medicine*, 41, 261–266.

Meltzer, H., Corbin, T., Gatward, R., Goodman, R. and Ford, T. (2003) *The Mental Health of Young People Looked After by Local Authorities in England*. London: HMSO..

Meltzer, H., Corbin, T., Gatward, R., Goodman, R. and Ford, T. (2004) *The Mental Health of Young People Looked After by Local Authorities in England*. London: National Statistics.

Meltzer, H., Gatward, R., Goodman, R. and Ford, T. (2000) *Mental Health of Children and Adolecsents in Great Britain*. London: HMSO.

Mendes, P. (2009) 'Improving outcomes for teenage pregnancy and early parenthood for young people in out-of-home care: a review of the literature.' *Youth Studies Australia*, 28, 3, 11–18.

Mendes, P., Johnson, G. and Moslehuddin, B. (2011) *Young People Leaving State Out-of-Home Care, Australian Policy and Practice*. Melbourne: Australian Scholarly Publishing.

Milham, S., Bullock, R., Hosie, K. and Haak, M. (1986) *Lost in Care*. Aldershot: Gower.

Miller, S. and Sweetman, L. (2007) *Making the Difference: Putting the Care Back into Corporate Parenting*. London: WMTD, Rainer and NCB.

Mooney, M., Statham, J., Monck, M. and Chambers, H. (2009) *Promoting the Health of Looked After Children, a Study to Inform Revision of the 2002 Guidance*. Research Report DCSF-RR125. London: Department for Children, Schools and Families.

Morgan, R. (2009a) *Children's Care Monitor 2009: Children on the State of Social Care in England Reported by the Children's Rights Director for England*. London: Ofsted.

Morgan, R. (2009b) *Children's Messages to the Minister: a Report on Children's Contributions to the 2009 Ministerial Stocktake of Care, by the Children's Rights Director for England*. London: Ofsted.

Morgan, R. and Lindsay, M. (2006) *Young People's Views on Leaving Care: What Young People in, and Formerly in, Residential and Foster Care Think About Leaving Care*. Newcastle upon Tyne: Commission for Social Care Inspection.

Morgan, R. and Lindsay, M. (2012) *Young People's Views on Care and Aftercare*. Office of the Children's Rights Director. London: Ofsted.

Morgan-Klein, B. (1985) *Where Am I Going to Stay?* Edinburgh: Scottish Council for Single Homeless.

Morris, J. (2002) *Moving Into Adulthood: Young Disabled People Moving Into Adulthood*. York: Joseph Rowntree Foundation.

Mulvey, T. (1977) 'After-care – who cares?' *Concern*, No. 26. London: National Children's Bureau.

Munro, E.R., Lushey, C., National Care Advisory Service, Maskell-Graham, D. and Ward, H. with Holmes, L. (2012) *Evaluation of the Staying Put: 18+ Family Placement Programme Pilot: Final Report*. Loughborough: Centre for Child and Family Research, Loughborough University.

Munro, E.R., Lushey, C., Ward, H. and National Care Advisory Service (2011) *Evaluation of the Right2BCared4 Pilots: Final Report*. Research Brief, Department for Education. RB106. London: Department for Education.

Munro, E.R., Pinkerton, J., Mendes, P., Hyde-Dryden, G., Herczog, M. and Benbenishty, R. (2011) 'The contribution of the United Nations Convention on the Rights of the Child to understanding and promoting the interests of young people making the transition from care to adulthood.' *Children and Youth Service Review*, 33, 12, 2417–2423.

NACRO (2005) *Reducing Offending for Looked After Children*. London: NACRO.

Nandy, S. and Selwyn, J. (2011) *Spotlight on Kinship Care, Using Census Microdata to Examine the Extent and Nature of Kinship Care in the UK*. Bristol: University of Bristol.

National Care Advisory Service (2008) *Introduction to Leaving Care*. London: NCAS.

National Care Advisory Service (2009) *Journeys to Home: Care Leavers' Successful Transition to Independent Accommodation*. London: NCAS.

National Care Advisory Service (2010a) *What is 'Suitable' Accommodation? Summary of NCAS Survey on how to Define Suitable Accommodation for Care Leavers.* London: NCAS.

National Care Advisory Service (2010b) *What Could Make the Difference? Care Leavers and the Welfare Benefits System.* London: NCAS.

National Care Advisory Service (2011a) *Making the Cut: Planning Transitions for Care Leavers in an Age of Austerity.* London: NCAS.

National Care Advisory Service (2011b) *Statistical Briefing: Looked-After Children and Care Leavers.* London: NCAS.

National Care Advisory Service (2011c) *From Care2Work, Phase 1 Final Report.* London: NCAS.

National Care Advisory Service (2011d) *From Care2Work, Monitoring Summary, April–September 2011.* London: NCAS.

National Care Advisory Service (2012) *Access All Areas: Action for All Government Departments to Support Young People's Journey from Care to Adulthood.* London: NCAS.

National Foster Care Association (2000) *Rights of Passage: Young Disabled People, the Transition from Foster Care to Adult Life: aStudy of Young People with Learning Difficulties.* London: National Foster Care Association.

NCB (2011a) *Open Public Services White Paper.* NCB Member Briefing. London: NCB.

NCB (2011b) *ARC Guide for Services – Supporting Disabled Young People from Black and Minority Ethnic Communities Through the Transition to Adulthood.* London: NCB.

NCB (2012) *Positive for Youth: a New Approach to Cross-Government Policy for Young People Aged 13–19.* NCB Member Briefing. London: NCB.

NCVYS (The National Council for Voluntary Youth Services) (2011) *Payment by Results and Social Investment, Briefing Paper.* London: NCVYS.

Newman, T. (2004) *What Works in Building Resilience?* Barkingside: Barnardo's.

Newman, T. and Blackburn, S. (2002) *Transitions in the Lives of Children and Young People: Resilience Factors.* Interchange 78. Edinburgh: Scottish Executive.

Newburn, T., Ward, J. and Pearson, G. (2002) *Drug Use Among Young People in Care.* Research Briefing 7. London: Economic and Social Research Council.

NICE and SCIE (2010) *Promoting the Quality of Life of Looked-after Children and Young People.* NICE Public Health Guidance 28. London: National Institute for Health and Clinical Excellence and Social Care Institute for Excellence.

Ofsted (2009) *Support for Care Leavers.* London: Ofsted.

Ofsted (2010) *An Evaluation of the Provision of Mental Health Services for Looked After Young People Over the Age of 16 Accommodated in Residential Settings.* London: Ofsted.

Ofsted (2011) *Children on Independent Reviewing Officers.* A report by the Children's Rights Director for England. London: Ofsted.

Packman, J. (1981) *The Child's Generation.* London: Blackwell and Robertson.

Page, R. and Clark, G. (eds) (1977) *Who Cares? Young People in Care Speak Out.* London: National Children's Bureau.

Park, J.M., Metraux, S., Broadbar, G. and Culhane, D.P. (2004) 'Public shelter admission among young adults with child welfare histories by type of service and type of exit.' *Social Service Review,* 78, 2, 284–303.

Parton, N. (1985) *The Politics of Child Abuse.* London: Macmillan.

Pearce, J.J. (2011) 'Working with trafficked children and young people: complexities in practice.' *British Journal of Social Work,* 41, 1424–1441.

Pearson, G. (1975) *The Deviant Imagination.* London: Macmillan.

Petrie, P., Boddy, J., Cameron, C., Simon, A. and Wigfall, V. (2006) *Working with Children in Europe.* Buckingham: Open University Press.

Pinkerton, J. (2006) 'Developing a global approach to the theory and practice of young people leaving state care.' *Child and Family Social Work,* 11, 3, 191–198.

Pinkerton, J. (2008) States of Care Leaving, Towards International Exchange as a Global Resource.' In M. Stein and E. Munro (eds) *Young People's Transitions from Care to Adulthood: International Research and Practice.* London: Jessica Kingsley.

Pinkerton, J. (2011) 'Constructing a global understanding of the social ecology of leaving out of home care.' *Children and Youth Services Review,* 33, 12, 2412–2416.

Pinkerton, J. and McCrea, J. (1999) *Meeting the Challenge? Young People Leaving Care in Northern Ireland.* Aldershot: Ashgate.

Priestley, M., Rabiee, P. and Harris, J. (2003) 'Young disabled people and the "new arrangements" for leaving care in England and Wales.' *Children and Youth Services Review,* 25, 11, 863–890.

Quilgars, D., Fitzpatrick, S. and Pleace, N. (2011) *Ending Youth Homelessness: Possibilities, Challenges and Practical Solutions.* Executive summary. London: Centerpoint.

Rabiee, P., Priestley, M. and Knowles, J. (2001) *Whatever Next? Young Disabled People Leaving Care.* Leeds: First Key.

Rainer (2007) *Home Alone: Housing and Support for Young People Leaving Care.* London: Rainer.

Rees, G., Stein, M., Hicks, L. and Gorin, S. (2011) *Adolescent Neglect: Research, Policy and Practice.* London: Jessica Kingsley Publishers.

Refugee Council (2005) *Ringing the Changes: the Impact of Guidance on the Use of Sections 17 and 20 of the Children Act 1989 to Support Unaccompanied Asylum Seeking Children.* London: The Refugee Council.

Ridge, T. and Millar, J. (2000) 'Excluding children: autonomy, friendship and the experience of the care system.' *Social Policy and Administration,* 34, 2, 160–175.

Ridley, J. and McCluskey, S. (2003) 'Exploring the perceptions of young people in care and care leavers of their health needs.' *Scottish Journal of Residential Childcare,* l2, 1.

Rutter, M. (1999) 'Resilience concepts and findings: implications for family therapy.' *Journal of Family Therapy,* 21, 119–144.

Rutter, M., Giller, H. and Hagell, A. (1998) *Antisocial Behaviour by Young People.* Cambridge: Cambridge University Press.

Samuels, G.M. and Pryce, J.M. (2008) ''What doesn't kill you makes you stronger': survivalist self-reliance as resilience and risk among young adults aging out of foster care.' *Children and Youth Services Review,* 30, 1198–1210.

Santayana, G. (1913) *Winds of Doctrine, Modernism and Christianity.* London: J.M. Dent.

Saunders, L. and Broad, B. (1997) *The Health Needs of Young People Leaving Care.* Leicester: De Montfort University.

Savage, T. (ed.) (2009) *Profiling London's Rough Sleepers: A Longitudinal Study of CHAIN Data.* London: Broadway Homeless and Support.

Schofield, G. (2001) 'Resilience and family placement: a lifespan perspective.' *Adoption and Fostering* 25, 3, 6–19.

Schofield, G. (2002) 'The significance of a secure base: a psychosocial model of long-term foster care.' *Child and Family Social Work,* 7, 4 259–272.

Schofield, G. and Beek, M. (2006) *Attachment Handbook for Foster Care and Adoption.* London: BAAF.

Schofield, G., Ward, E., Biggart, L., Scaife, V. *et al.* (2012) *Looked After Children and Offending: Reducing Risk and Promoting Resilience.* Norwich: Centre for Research on the Child and Family, UEA and TACT.

Scotland's Commissioner for Children and Young People (2008) *Sweet 16? The Age of Leaving Care in Scotland. Report to the Scottish Parliament.* Edinburgh: SCCYP.

Scottish Council for Single Homeless (SCSH) (1981) *Think Single.* Edinburgh: SCSH.

Scottish Health Feedback (2001) *A Study of the Health Needs of Young People with Experience of Being in Care in Glasgow.* Glasgow: The Big Step.

Scottish Health Feedback (2003) *The Health Needs and Issues of Young People from Glasgow Living in Foster Care Settings.* Glasgow: The Big Step.

Sempik, J., Ward, H. and Darker, I. (2008) 'Emotional and behavioural difficulties of children and young people at entry into care.' *Clinical Child Psychology and Psychology and Psychiatry*, 13, 2, 221–233.

Shaw, C. (1998) *Remember my Messages: the Experiences and Views of 200 Children in Public Care.* London: The Who Cares? Trust.

Simon, A. (2008) 'Early access and use of housing: care leavers and other young people in difficulty.' *Child and Family Social Work*, 13, 1, 91–100.

Sinclair, I., Baker, C., Lee, J. and Gibbs, I. (2007) *The Pursuit of Permanence: a Study of the English Care System.* London: Jessica Kingsley Publishers.

Sinclair, I., Baker, C., Wilson, K. and Gibbs, I. (2003) *What Happens to Foster Children? Report to the Department of Health.* York: University of York.

Sinclair, I., Baker, C., Wilson, K. and Gibbs, I. (2005) *Foster Children, Where They Go and How They Get On.* London: Jessica Kingsley Publishers.

Sinclair, I. and Gibbs, I. (1998) *Children's Homes: a Study in Diversity.* Chichester: Wiley.

Sirriyeh, A. (2011) 'Research: good practice when working with refugee and asylum seeking children.' *Community Care*, 15 April, 6694, 1–3.

Skuse, T., Macdonald, I. and Ward, H. (2001) *Looking After Children: Transforming Data into Management Information.* Report of longitudinal study at 30 September 1999, third interim report to the Department of Health. Loughborough: Centre for Child and Family Research, Loughborough University.

Slesnick, N. and Meade, M. (2001) 'System youth: a subgroup of substance-abusing homeless adolescents.' *Journal of Substance Abuse*, 13, 3, 367–384.

Sloper, P., Beecham, J., Clarke, S., Franklin, A., Moran, N. and Cusworth, L. (2011) 'Transition to adult services for disabled young people and those with complex health needs.' *Research Works*, 2011–02. York: Social Policy Research Unit, University of York.

Smith, B.W. (2011) *Youth Leaving Foster Care: a Developmental Relationship-Based Approach to Practice* Oxford: Oxford University Press.

Social Exclusion Unit (1998) *Rough Sleeping.* London: HMSO.

Social Exclusion Unit (1999) *Teenage Pregnancy.* London: HMSO.

Social Exclusion Unit (2002) *Young Runaways.* London: SEU.

Social Exclusion Unit (2003) *A Better Education for Children in Care.* London: HMSO.

Stanley, K. (2001) *Cold Comfort: Young Separated Refugees in England.* London: Save the Children.

Stein, M. (1990) *Living Out of Care.* Barkingside: Barnardo's.

Stein, M. (1991) *Leaving Care and the 1989 Children Act: the Agenda.* Leeds: First Key.

Stein, M. (1999) 'Leaving Care: Reflections and challenges.' In O. Stevenson (ed.) *Child Welfare in the UK.* Oxford: Blackwell.

Stein, M. (2004) *What Works for Young People Leaving Care?* Barkingside: Barnardo's.

Stein, M. (2005) *Resilience and Young People Leaving Care: Overcoming the Odds.* York: Joseph Rowntree Foundation.

Stein, M. (2006a) 'Missing years of abuse in children's homes.' *Child and Family Social Work*, 11, 11–21.

Stein, M. (2006b) 'Research review: young people leaving care.' *Child and Family Social Work*, 11, 3, 273–279.

Stein, M. (2006c) 'Young people aging out of care: the poverty of theory.' *Children and Youth Services Review*, 28, 422–435.

Stein, M. (2008a) 'Resilience and young people leaving care.' *Child Care in Practice*, 14, 1, 35–44.

Stein, M. (2008b) 'The making of leaving care policy 1971–2008.' *Youth and Policy*, 100, 241–251.

Stein, M. (2009a) 'Young People Leaving Care.' In G. Schofield and J. Simmonds (eds) *The Child Placement Handbook: Research, Policy and Practice*. London: British Association for Adoption and Fostering.

Stein, M. (2009b) *Quality Matters in Children's Services: Messages from Research*. London: Jessica Kingsley Publishers.

Stein, M. (2011) *Care Less Lives, the Story of the Rights Movement of Young People in Care*. London: Catch-22.

Stein, M. and Carey, K. (1986) *Leaving Care*. Oxford: Blackwell.

Stein, M and Dumaret, A.-C. (2011) 'The mental health of young people aging out of care and entering adulthood: exploring the evidence from England and France.' *Children and Youth Services Review*, 33,12, 2504–2511.

Stein, M. and Ellis, S (1983) *Gizza Say: Reviews and Young People in Care*. London: NAYPIC.

Stein, M. and Maynard, C. (1985) *I've Never Been So Lonely*. London: NAYPIC.

Stein, M. and Morris, M. (2010) *Increasing the Numbers of Care Leavers in 'Settled, Safe' Accommodation*. Vulnerable Children Knowledge Review 3. London: C4EO.

Stein, M. and Munro, E. (eds) (2008) *Young People's Transitions from Care to Adulthood: International Research and Practice*. London: Jessica Kingsley Publishers.

Stein, M., Pinkerton, J. and Kelleher, J. (2000) 'Young people leaving care in England, Northern Ireland, and Ireland.' *European Journal of Social Work*, 3, 3, 235–246.

Stein, M. and Wade, J. (2000) *Helping Care Leavers: Problems and Strategic Responses*. London: Department of Health.

Stein, M., Ward H. and Courtney, M. (2011) 'Editorial: international perspectives on young people's transitions from care to adulthood.' *Children and Youth Services Review*, 33,12, 2409–2411.

Stone, M. (1990) *Young People Leaving Care*. Redhill: The Royal Philanthropic Society.

Taylor, C. (2003) 'Social Work and Looked After Children.' In D.B. Smith (ed.) *Evidenced-Based Practice*. London: Jessica Kingsley Publishers.

Thomas, S., Nafees, B. and Bhugra, D. (2004) '"I was running away from death' – the pre-flight experiences of unaccompanied asylum seeking children in the UK.' *Child Care, Health and Development*, 30, 2, 113–122.

Tilbury, C., Creed, P., Buys, N. and Meegan, C. (2011) 'The school to work transition for young people in state care: perspectives from young people, carers and professionals.' *Child and Family Social Work*, 16, 345–352.

Utting, W. (1991) *Children in Public Care: a Review of Residential Child Care*. London: HMSO.

Utting, W. (1997) *People Like Us: the Report of the Review of the Safeguards for Children Living Away From Home*. London: HMSO.

Vasillou, C. and Ryrie, I. (2006) 'Someone there to talk to.' *Mental Health Today*, October, 23–26.

Vernon, J. (2000) *Audit and Assessment of Leaving Care Services in London*. London: NCB.

Vinnerljung, B., Franzen, E. and Danielsson, M. (2007) 'Teenage parenthood among child welfare clients: a Swedish national cohort study of prevalence and odds.' *Journal of Adolescence*, 30, 97–116.

Wade, J. (2008) 'The ties that bind: support from birth families and substitute families for young people leaving care.' *British Journal of Social Work*, 38, 1, 39–54.

Wade, J. (2011) 'Preparation and transition planning for unaccompanied asylum-seeking and refugee young people: a review of evidence in England.' *Children and Youth Services Review*, 33, 12, 2424–2430.

Wade, J., Biehal, N., Farrelly, N. and Sinclair, I. (2011) *Caring for Abused and Neglected Children: Making the Right Decisions for Reunification or Long-term Care*. London: Jessica Kingsley Publishers.

Wade, J. and Dixon, J. (2006) 'Making a home, finding a job: investigating early housing and employment outcomes for young people leaving care.' *Child and Family Social Work*, 11, 3, 199–208.

Wade, J., Mitchell, F. and Baylis, G. (2005) *Unaccompanied Asylum Seeking Children: the Response of Social Work Services.* London: BAAF.

Ward, H. (2011) 'Continuities and discontinuities: issues concerning the establishment of a persistent sense of self amongst care leavers.' *Children and Youth Services Review,* 33, 12, 2512–2518.

Ward, J., Henderson, Z. and Pearson, G. (2003) *One Problem Among Many: Drug Use Among Care Leavers in Transition to Independent Living.* Home Office Research Study 260. London: Home Office.

Ward, H. and Skuse, T. (2001) 'Performance targets and stability of placements for children looked after away from home.' *Children and Society,* 15, 333–346.

Who Cares? Trust (1993) *Not Just a Name: the Views of Young People in Foster and Residential Care.* London: National Consumer Council.

WMTD (2008) *Making the Difference. Putting the Care Back Into Corporate Parenting. A Practical Guide for Local Authorities as Corporate Parents.* London: Rainer.

Wolmar, C (1980) 'Out of care.' *Roof,* March/April, London: Shelter.

York Consulting Limited (2007) *Evaluation of the Columba 1400 Careleaver Programme. Final Report.* Edinburgh: Scottish Executive. Available at www.scotland.gov.uk/Resource/Doc/168892/0046968.pdf, accessed on 5 March 2012.

Youth Justice Board (2007) *Accommodation Needs and Experiences.* London: Youth Justice Board.

Zeira, A. and Benbenishty, R. (2011) 'Readiness for independent living of adolescents in youth villages in Israel.' *Children and Youth Services Review,* 33, 12, 2461–2468.

Subject Index

Author Index